ECO-RESORTS: PLANNING AND DESIGN FOR THE TROPICS

Zbigniew Bromberek

AMSTERDAM • BOSTON • HEIDELBERG • LONDON • NEW YORK • OXFORD
PARIS • SAN DIEGO • SAN FRANCISCO • SYDNEY • TOKYO

Architectural Press is an imprint of Elsevier

ELSEVIER

Architectural Press

Architectural Press is an imprint of Elsevier
Linacre House, Jordan Hill, Oxford OX2 8DP, UK
30 Corporate Drive, Suite 400, Burlington, MA 01803, USA

First edition 2009

British Library Cataloguing in Publication Data
A catalogue record for this book is available from the British Library

Library of Congress Cataloguing in Publication Data
A catalogue record for this book is available from the Library of Congress

ISBN: 978-0-7506-5793-8

For information on all Architectural Press publications
visit our web site at www.architecturalpress.com

Printed and bound in UK

09 10 10 9 8 7 6 5 4 3 2 1

Contents

About this book   ix

Acknowledgements   x

List of figures   xi

Part One • Eco-tourism and the Tropics

1.0   A question of sustainability   3
1.1   Tropical tourism and tropical eco-tourism: scale and trends   7
1.2   Delineation of the tropics   11
    1.2.1   Tropical climates and the building   12
    1.2.2   Ecology of the tropics   18
1.3   Operational issues in eco-friendly resort design   21
    1.3.1   Energy management   23
    1.3.2   Water management   30
    1.3.3   Waste and pollution management   32
    1.3.4   Impact of building materials and construction technology   35
    1.3.5   Impacts from tourist presence in the area   39
1.4   Eco-tourism rating schemes   43

Part Two • Indoor Environment Control in the Tropics

2.0   A question of comfort   47
2.1   Thermal environment control   53
    2.1.1   Heat flows   57
    2.1.2   Air movement   69
    2.1.3   Humidity   76
2.2   Visual environment control   79
    2.2.1   Artificial lighting systems appropriate for a tropical eco-resort   86
2.3   Acoustic environment control   87
    2.3.1   Noise pollution and effective countermeasures   88
2.4   Control of smell, touch and psychological factors in environmental perceptions   91

Part Three • Tropical Eco-resort Design

3.0	A question of environmental response	95
3.1	Location	99
3.2	Site planning	101
	3.2.1 Hill influence	101
	3.2.2 Sea influence	101
	3.2.3 Vegetation influence	102
	3.2.4 Spatial organisation	102
3.3	Constructional design	109
3.4	Building design	111
	3.4.1 Building layout	111
	3.4.2 Envelope design	112
	3.4.3 Building fabric	121
3.5	Functional programmes	129
3.6	Room design	133
3.7	Resort operation in planning and design objectives	137

Part Four • Case studies

4.0	A question of practicality	141
4.1	Jean-Michel Cousteau Fiji Islands Resort	145
	4.1.1 In their own words	145
	4.1.2 Site selection and landscaping	146
	4.1.3 Construction and materials	146
	4.1.4 Energy management	147
	4.1.5 Water management	147
	4.1.6 Waste management	149
	4.1.7 The control of other impacts	149
	4.1.8 The resort's climatic performance	150
	4.1.9 Concluding remarks	151
4.2	Are Tamanu Beach Hotel and Muri Beach Hideaway	153
	4.2.1 In their own words	153
	4.2.2 Site selection and landscaping	153
	4.2.3 Construction and materials	154
	4.2.4 Energy management	156
	4.2.5 Water management	159
	4.2.6 Waste management	160
	4.2.7 The resort's climatic performance	160
	4.2.8 Concluding remarks	160
4.3	Sheraton Moorea Lagoon Resort & Spa	163
	4.3.1 In their own words	163
	4.3.2 Site selection and landscaping	163
	4.3.3 Construction	163
	4.3.4 Operational energy	166
	4.3.5 Water management	166
	4.3.6 Waste management	166
	4.3.7 The resort's climatic performance	166
	4.3.8 Concluding remarks	169
4.4	Bora Bora Nui Resort & Spa	173
	4.4.1 In their own words	173
	4.4.2 Site selection and landscaping	176

Contents

4.4.3	Construction	176
4.4.4	Operational energy	176
4.4.5	Water management	178
4.4.6	Waste management	178
4.4.7	The resort's climatic performance	178
4.4.8	Concluding remarks	178
4.5	**Mezzanine**	185
4.5.1	In their own words	185
4.5.2	Site selection and landscaping	186
4.5.3	Construction	187
4.5.4	Energy management	187
4.5.5	Water management	188
4.5.6	Waste management	188
4.5.7	The resort's climatic performance	188
4.5.8	Concluding remarks	192
4.6	**Balamku Inn on the Beach**	193
4.6.1	In their own words	193
4.6.2	Site selection and landscaping	196
4.6.3	Construction	196
4.6.4	Energy management	197
4.6.5	Water management	199
4.6.6	Waste management	199
4.6.7	The resort's climatic performance	200
4.6.8	Concluding remarks	200
4.7	**KaiLuumcito the Camptel**	203
4.7.1	Site selection and landscaping	203
4.7.2	Construction	203
4.7.3	Energy management	207
4.7.4	Water management	207
4.7.5	Waste management	209
4.7.6	The resort's climatic performance	209
4.7.7	Concluding remarks	210
4.8	**Hacienda Chichén Resort**	211
4.8.1	Site selection and landscaping	211
4.8.2	Construction	213
4.8.3	Energy management	213
4.8.4	Water management	213
4.8.5	Waste management	213
4.8.6	The resort's climatic performance	214
4.8.7	Concluding remarks	214
Bibliography		217
Index		229

About this book

At the time of writing this book society faces a looming problem of global warming, seen by many as the consequence of ignoring warning signs over many years of industrialisation. It appears that emissions of carbon dioxide and other civilisation by-products into the atmosphere have added to other factors with disastrous effect for the entire world. In truth, the signs of global warming have come upon us more quickly than even the pessimists could have predicted. Yet, we do not actually know what causes global warming – we can at best take an educated guess. The fact remains, though, that global warming is a reality.

In our field of architecture, we could be contributing to the environmental problems facing the planet more than others. We have known for many years that we should be paying greater heed to the way we design and construct, so that the resultant impact on the environment is minimal. Building is an irreversible activity, leaving – directly and indirectly – a permanent mark on the Earth. Yet we choose simplistic solutions to complex problems and we let economic imperatives override any pricking of the conscience that our current design practices might be generating. With the new awareness of the world that we are gaining through intensive scientific studies, we have a duty to understand the ramifications of what we are doing.

We are part of the world – an important part, yes, but only a part. Most of our present-day efforts to achieve 'sustainability', as I see them, are anthropocentric and inherently flawed. They are a highly tangible manifestation of our interference with systems we know very little about. At the moment, we apply our limited knowledge to preserve what we believe is worth having – according to our own priorities, presumed importance or perceived needs. There is something fundamentally wrong with even a mere suggestion that we improve the world.

Indeed, the very notion of 'improving' the world seems bizarre: improving it for whom or for what? Unless, that is, we are prepared to openly admit that we are not doing it for the world in its entirety, but for ourselves and ourselves only – in our selfish and egocentric pursuit of our current convictions. Nothing more and nothing less...

This book is about planning and design in one of the most fragile environments on Earth: the tropics. It does not offer, least prescribe, solutions that would deliver a sustainable outcome. Nevertheless, it does invite using caution to protect what remains unchanged and to build in a way that makes as little impact as possible. It asks you to make good use of existing local resources before reaching for more of them, further away from the places of their use. It also argues that we should take only what we really need from this environment, leaving the rest untouched. Inherent in eco-tourism is the paradox of drawing on pristine environments and thus causing the inevitable loss of their principal quality: their unspoilt purity.

I would like to see all eco-resort developers in the tropics tread lightly, eco-resort operators and users to scale down their demands and adapt to the conditions, and eco-resort planners and designers to utilise the acquired knowledge in drafting their responses to the tropical setting. I would advocate a broad use of the precautionary principle: a process in which we weigh up the long-term consequences of our actions, refraining from, or at least limiting, activities that may cause irreversible change. We must proceed cautiously because, even with the best intentions, it is possible that actions we take now, well-informed as they may now seem to be, may in future turn out to be deleterious to the environment. Together, using this respectful and considerate approach, we can save the beauty and diversity of the tropics for ourselves and for the generations to come.

Zbigniew Bromberek

Figures 4.5.10–11   Room height allows for vertical air movement and sensible cooling through stack effect ventilation making the indoor environment thermally comfortable

Figure 4.5.12   The two parts of the resort – the guest unit one (on the left) and restaurant/office (on the right) – are separated, which, together with background noise from the breaking waves, ensures favourable acoustic conditions

Figure 4.5.13   The extent of the resort's potential environmental impacts. (Note: The extent of the resort's impacts [ranging from positive through neutral to negative] should be read in conjunction with the information in Figure 4.1)

Figure 4.6.1   Balamku Inn comprises guest units housed in single- and double-storey buildings

Figure 4.6.2   Plan of the resort

Figure 4.6.3   The largest building contains the reception, resort dining room and kitchen, with the office and owner/operator accommodation on the upper floor

Figures 4.6.4–5   Second-storey units benefit from high cathedral ceilings allowing hot air to rise under the roof; ground floor units have their thermal environment shaped by the openness of the plan and staying permanently in the 'shade' of the upper floor

Figure 4.6.6   The resort's dining room has substantial thermal mass and stays comfortably cool even in hot weather conditions

Figure 4.6.7   A 'mosquito magnet', which attracts and captures mosquitoes, helps to control the insect problem on site

Figure 4.6.8   Small on-demand hot water heater

Figure 4.6.9   Positioning a holding tank on the roof provides gravity, thus pressurising the system

Figure 4.6.10   Each building has its own composting toilet unit

Figure 4.6.11   The created wetlands are used for purifying grey water from sinks and showers

Figure 4.6.12   Rooms are decorated with work by local artisans

Figures 4.6.13–14   Resort buildings are built relatively close to each other leaving a large tract of land reserved for the resort's conservation effort

Figure 4.6.15   The extent of the resort's potential environmental impacts. (Note: The extent of resort's impacts [ranging from positive through neutral to negative] should be read in conjunction with the information in Figure 4.1)

Figure 4.7.1   The super-low weight of KaiLuumcito structures allows them to sit right on the beach

Figure 4.7.2   The main reason for bringing the resort to its current site was the natural lagoon and its wildlife

Figures 4.7.3–4   The KaiLuumcito accommodation is provided in tentalapas – a combination of specially designed tents shaded by palapas (traditional Mexican roofed structures without walls)

Figures 4.7.5–6   The resort structures have been erected using traditional local building techniques and the expertise of the local labour force

Figure 4.7.7   The resort's lounge in the main *palapa* has walls made with sticks arranged to provide visual privacy of the area

Figures 4.7.8–9   Toilet blocks are rather conventional except for lighting, which comes from oil lamps; washing rooms are external parts of the toilet block entirely open to the air

Figure 4.7.10   Diesel torches are lit at dusk and provide lighting until fuel burns out

Figure 4.7.11   All structures at the resort utilise natural materials in their simplest unprocessed form

List of figures

Figure 4.7.12   General view of the KaiLuumcito shows both toilet blocks and a file of
                    tentalapas along the beach

Figures 4.7.13–14   Both the kitchen and the dining hall are housed in the main palapa of
                    the resort; neither room has walls

Figure 4.7.15   The history of KaiLuumcito commenced in 1976; the resort has been
                    devastated several times by major cyclones and has required rebuilding

Figure 4.7.16   The extent of the resort's potential environmental impacts. (Note: The
                    extent of resort's impacts [ranging from positive through neutral to
                    negative] should be read in conjunction with the information in Figure 4.1)

Figure 4.8.1   The resort's main draw card is the fact that it is located next to the world
                    famous Mayan ruins of Chichén Itzá

Figures 4.8.2–3   Accommodation at the resort is offered in buildings that housed the
                    1920s archaeological expedition to the area; the structures were erected
                    chiefly with stone recovered from the ancient city

Figure 4.8.4   The buildings have been 'recycled': the original building envelope was
                    retrofitted with all modern conveniences and the interior brought up to
                    modern standards

Figure 4.8.5   The single-line tram was used by early twentieth-century tourists and
                    awaits restoration

Figure 4.8.6   Al fresco dining is offered at the main house of the Hacienda, which was
                    built for its Spanish owners in the eighteenth century

Figure 4.8.7   The change of character from a former cattle ranch to a tourist resort is
                    most visible in the landscaping design; view from the restaurant deck
                    towards one of the accommodation buildings

Figure 4.8.8   The Hacienda has undertaken a massive effort of re-vegetating degraded
                    parts of the property with indigenous plants, giving employment to the
                    local villagers in the process

Figure 4.8.9   The property has its own historic attractions including a small church
                    built by the Spaniards in the seventeenth century

Figure 4.8.10   The extent of the resort's potential environmental impacts. (Note: The
                    extent of resort's impacts [ranging from positive through neutral to
                    negative] should be read in conjunction with the information in Figure 4.1)

Part One
Eco-tourism and the Tropics

The world's tropical zone extends to approximately 4000 km north and 3500 km south of the equator and covers one third of the Earth's land surface: in total it takes in over 50 million square kilometres. Globally, the tropical lands have a coastline of over 60 000 kilometres attracting millions of tourists every year with these numbers rising dramatically in recent times. Consequently, more tourist and recreational infrastructure in the tropics is increasingly needed and tourist resorts have started moving also into previously undeveloped areas.

Meanwhile, up until the 1980s, the emphasis of any tourist development in the tropics was on primary resources, such as the beach and the sea; the contribution which accommodation can make to successful holidays was neglected. This situation has obviously changed. Facilities built for tourists have to be designed to cope with the climatic stress of the tropics yet must provide a lifestyle compatible with tourists' requirements, and do it in the most economical way. Furthermore, although a vast majority of the travellers come from developed countries, most tourist-attracting tropical areas are in developing countries of the third world.

This dichotomy causes or contributes to many undesirable phenomena that follow tourism developments in such regions. And yet, many of them seem easily avoidable by correct interpretation of, and response to, the visitors' expectations. Ever increasing portions amongst them are tourists who want to get closer to the nature and culture of the region whilst at the same time being conscious of the need to preserve what is left of it. This desire gave rise to the eco-tourism movement more than 30 years ago. Today eco-tourism is coming of age, being the fastest growing segment of the tourist industry. Our environmental concerns are more and more often reflected in choices that we make about the way we spend our holidays. Eco-tourism is an expression of this trend.

The events surrounding the last of a three-decade long series of nuclear tests in French Polynesia clearly demonstrated a heightened environmental awareness in the region and in the world. In Australia, an attempt to develop a resort in an environmentally sensitive area of the Whitsunday Passage met with a similar reaction of concern from the public. These stories are repeated around the tropical world, from Yucatan to Borneo and from the Bahamas to the Amazon basin. Nevertheless, it seems unlikely that developments, and tourist developments in particular, in all sensitive environments will be stopped or prevented. In some of them, and eventually in most of them, tourist infrastructure will be developed. This will, most certainly, be followed by unavoidable impacts, which these establishments will make, on the environment. It is up to resort planners, designers and operators to make such impacts the least possible or, at the very minimum, the least damaging.

It is said that architecture reflects needs, desires, customs, attitudes and aspirations present in society. There are then a number of reasons for which eco-tourist resorts should display an environment-friendly attitude. An efficient passive climate control, providing indoor environmental comfort in the resort, could effectively propagate solutions based broadly on non-powered passive techniques. Many tourists, and certainly the vast majority of eco-tourists, would be happy to try to adjust to the given climate conditions at the holiday destination they have chosen. It is not true that the tropical climate is unbearable. It is equally not true that passive architecture cannot cope with the conditions found in the tropics. Passive climate control will not secure constant low temperature as powered air-conditioning can do. However, the need for constant temperature is at least questionable. Adaptation is apparently much healthier than desperate efforts to insulate the building and its occupants from climatic impacts. It is also much healthier and more sustainable. Much more can also be done to integrate tourist developments with the cultural heritage of their hosting regions, their customs and social fabric.

New trends in global tourism require that tourism developers in the tropics take an environmentally conscious stance if they do not want to undermine the base on which they operate. Developers of tropical resorts have to meet the demand to accommodate growing flows of people who arrive there with quite specific expectations. An important, if not rather obvious, observation to be made is that tourists go to a resort for leisure. They try to break away from their everyday work, everyday life and everyday environment. Tourists tend to contrast everything left behind with the time spent in the resort. Part of the holiday excitement is derived from experiencing the tropics indeed, the tropics as they really are, hot, often humid, and sometimes rainy as well. The provided accommodation should make that experience possible at a somewhat comfortable level – home levels of comfort are seldom required. Another obvious but often-overlooked fact is that visitors are very different from the local residents. Their expectations are driving their perceptions and have the ability of modifying them to a large extent. This fact could and should be utilised in the resort plan and design to work with the environment rather than against it.

1.0
A question of sustainability

Tourist facilities in the tropics, and eco-tourist facilities in particular, target very valuable and usually highly sensitive environments. For example, the greatest demand for tourist development opportunities in Australia can be seen on its eastern coast, from the central coast of New South Wales to Marlin coast (the coastal area near Cooktown) in the far north of Queensland. Concentrations of this demand build up pressure for extensive development in several locations, including the entire coastal strip in the tropics up to Daintree, Cooktown and Cape Melville National Park. While in the south of Australia the natural environment has been subjected to urbanisation for many years, in the tropics this type of modification has been introduced fairly late, in the last several years. In other words, the targeted tropical section of the coast in Australia remains its only unspoilt part, the only refuge for many endangered animals and the only remaining habitat for many endangered plants. This trend was also noted, and a response to it called for, by the Alliance of Small Island Developing States in its 1994 Barbados Programme for Action (WMO 1995). The same can be said about other parts of the world. The focus of tourist developments is nowadays firmly trained on previously untouched or undeveloped areas. Figure 1.1.

Apparently, there is an answer to this environmental dilemma and it is the 'ecologically sustainable (tourist) development'. Many definitions of ecologically sustainable development or ESD have been offered, some general and some more precise. The following definition, promoted by the United Nations, is also known as the 'Brundtland definition':

> [ESD] is development, which meets the needs of the present without compromising the ability of future generations to meet their own needs.

The concept of 'sustainability' is relatively new. The Bank of English, the database on which the first edition of Collins-COBUILD Dictionary of English was based in 1987, contained around 20 million words of written and spoken English of the 1980s. There was no mention of 'sustainable' let alone 'sustainability' among them. Both appear as low-frequency words in the 1995 edition of the Bank, based on a collection of 200 million words of the 1990s. Even the most recent (2006) edition of the dictionary does not define 'sustainability'. As a concept, is it still too early or too difficult to grasp, perhaps?

'Sustainability' is a term that represents a social and cultural shift in the world order. It has become a symbol describing this inevitable, ongoing transformation. As such, the term has little to do with the literal description or dictionary definition of the word, but is the name for a new attitude and new way of looking at the world. 'Sustainability' is also a concept increasingly used as a measure of worth – when it comes to evaluating the contemporary built environment. It appears that a lot of effort has been put into integrating various assessment techniques related to environment-friendly, energy-efficient buildings and developments as well as other activities involving management of natural resources under a banner of 'sustainability'.

More prudent approaches to the environment gain recognition and importance. Development methods and approaches have been changing worldwide to adopt the concept of sustainability into the planning and design of the built environment. To build, by definition, means to make a lasting impact on the environment. The challenge is to find a balance between the aesthetic and environmental needs of a project, as well as between tangible and intangible threats and opportunities, to secure increasingly scarce resources for future generations. Architecture these days more often than ever is judged as 'good architecture' as long as it provides a high quality environment that is cost-optimal and consistent with energy-efficiency at all stages of construction and use.

Users, owners, designers, constructors, and maintainers from all sectors are actively seeking techniques to create a built environment, which will efficiently use all resources and minimise waste, conserve the natural environment and create a healthy and durable built environment. Numerous sources offer principles of 'sustainable architecture' to guide and help architects.

Within the field of 'sustainable architecture', sustainability represents a transition to a 'more humane and natural' built environment. However, architecture, by its very nature, uses energy, alters the existing fabric and imposes its structural forms upon others. It will always have some detrimental impact on the environment. No active human-created system can

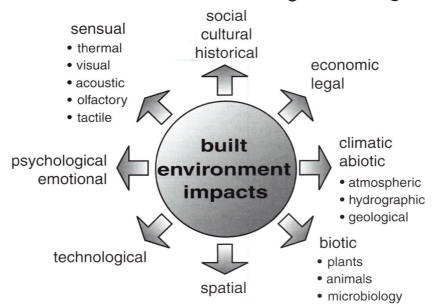

Figure 1.2 Various environments impacted on by the built environment.

sustainability issues but, at the same time, use a different vehicle to do it.

In the context of 'sustainability', 'sustain' does not mean that nothing ever changes. Nor does it mean that nothing bad ever happens. 'Sustainability' is not about maintaining the status quo or reaching perfection. 'Sustainable architecture', then, is a response to an awareness to pursue certain ideas and not a prescriptive formula for survival. In its literal meaning, it is a misnomer. Moreover, the integrity of the concept would be eroded if it were to have to rely on too many or overly prescriptive measures. 'Best practice' avoids this trap by relating to a constantly evolving set of solutions.

In architecture, 'best practice', for all practical purposes, is synonymous with 'sustainable' but easier to grasp and more beneficial in the long term, and should replace it as an environmental education vehicle. Nevertheless, architects should be made aware that in this profession these two terms are interchangeable and clients demanding 'sustainable design' in fact require that best practice objectives be followed and best practice solutions adopted.

New knowledge being generated in the area of sustainability will be forcing reviews of existing practices as long as we consider sustainability important. It is going to pose a challenge to resort designers and planners as well as architectural educators for many years to come. Instead of aiming at some abstract perpetual objective, the professionals we trust our future with need to promise to do the best they can – today and every day.

1.1

Tropical tourism and tropical eco-tourism: scale and trends

Leisure, as a tip of the triangle of life activities (dwelling–work–leisure), has been fast gaining in importance in recent years. Tourism and travel (T&T) is the world's fastest growing industry. Its contribution is soon expected to approach US$5 trillion or one-eighth of the world Gross Domestic Product (GDP). According to turn of the century forecasts from the World Tourism Organization, the number of international tourist arrivals is expected to reach 937 million by the year 2010 and 1600 million by 2020. Tropical regions will record the biggest growth. In a group of countries enjoying warm (subtropical and tropical) types of climate, tourism industries become increasingly important sectors of their economies. For quite a few of these countries, development of tourism and recreation services is a vital part of their survival strategies during cyclical periods of economic downturn. Tourism already generates 95 per cent of GDP in the Maldives and 75 per cent of export earnings in the Bahamas. Such growth in tourism is matched with a growing need for infrastructure and facilities, and this is where the problems start appearing. While tourism, no doubt, represents a huge stimulus to the global (and local) economy, it will also have a lasting impact on the global (and local) environment. Figure 1.3.

In search of variety and new sensations, tourists have started exploring even the most remote and inaccessible corners of the Earth. Increasing numbers of travellers seek natural and cultural locations which remain pristine. Numbers of visitors to national parks and protected areas, and to remote rural communities, continue to rise. Some of these regions are extremely important habitats, as they constitute the last refuges for endangered species. The importance of other locations is derived from their place in regional and/or global ecosystems. In the case of coastal tropics, the problem of protecting these habitats is exacerbated by their natural vulnerability. Any uncontrolled disturbance in such an environment has potentially disastrous consequences. Sports and leisure activities by their nature depend heavily on a healthy environment with high quality of air and water as a minimum prerequisite.

While nature based eco-tourism is generally considered to have a lower impact than typical mass tourism, requiring less infrastructure and development, even small-scale use can damage the natural resources, which attract tourists in the first place. There are also other effects, extending tourism's influence beyond the ecological impact. The best example is its socio-economic impact. Tourism, especially in rural and undeveloped areas, tends to create a dependence on foreign income among the local population. It displaces traditional customs and social interactions, and makes those communities vulnerable to foreign economic conditions. Degradation of the corals of the Great Barrier Reef, deforestation in the foothills of the Himalayas, disruption of feeding and breeding patterns of wildlife in Kenya's national parks, and the gradual dismantling of the Kalahari and Amazonian indigenous communities all serve as warnings to the potential dangers of uncontrolled tourism. Eco-tourism, with its focus on local nature and culture, should be a kind of 'import' that promises to explore those environments without destroying them. Figure 1.4.

Eco-tourism appears to be a value- (or philosophy-) laden approach to tourism, aiming at environmental sustainability. One has to ask, however, what is sustained (natural environment, culture, the activity itself) and how is it sustained (at what costs and benefits, and who is to benefit). The World Tourism Organization's Environment Committee established a task force to investigate the development of international sustainability indicators of tourism. The indicators, explained and described in the Indicators for the Sustainable Management of Tourism (1995), are designed to address links between the tourism industry and the environment, the impact of the industry on the environment, and the effects of social and natural environmental factors on the prosperity of the industry.

The participants at the World Conference on Sustainable Tourism, meeting in Spain in 1995, adopted the Charter for Sustainable Tourism (www.geocities. com). It recognised that tourism is ambivalent, since it can contribute positively to socio-economic and

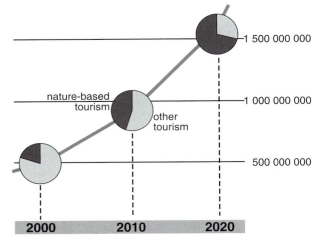

Figure 1.3 Tourist numbers globally and nature-based tourism market share.

cultural achievement, while at the same time it can also contribute to the degradation of the environment and the loss of local identity. It should be approached with a global methodology taking into account a simple truth that the resources, on which tourism is based, are fragile and that there is a growing demand for improved environmental quality. To be sustainable, tourism needs to meet economic expectations and environmental requirements, and respect not only the social and physical structure of destinations, but also the local population. In particular, the use of energy, tourism-related transport, the 'Triple R' (Reduce–Reuse–Recycle) and impact minimisation strategies in resorts should receive a great deal of attention.

As is the case with sustainability, there is no commonly agreed definition of 'eco-tourism'. This is because the general concept of eco-tourism (such as nature-based tourism or 'sustainable' tourism) itself is still a much-disputed topic. Eco-tourism can be defined as visiting relatively undisturbed places for enjoying biotic (fauna and flora) and abiotic components of the local environment. However, different experts tend to stress different aspects of eco-tourism: economic, social, cultural or others. Eco-tourism is supposed to have three main components: it is to be nature-based, sustainable (which also includes consideration of economic and socio-cultural impacts), and have educational/interpretative qualities. A scrutiny of these three components reveals that almost invariably financial costs of eco-tourism business endeavours, which operate in a way of making no more than negligible impacts on the environment and educating at the same time, tend to be higher than the generated income. This raises the chief concern about eco-tourism, which has a potential to develop into smaller forms of mass tourism. Examples of facilities practising environmental audits or monitoring schemes, where impacts can be identified, controlled and eventually minimised, are very rare indeed.

Nowadays, eco-tourism seems to be a very fashionable trend, which emphasises direct contact with nature, and protection and conservation of the natural environment. It is one of the two relatively new major trends that can be identified in the development of coastal resorts, the other being 'business tourism' (defined as the tourism related to professional/occupational activities of the traveller). The National Ecotourism Strategy, tabled by the Australian Commonwealth Department of Tourism defines eco-tourism as nature-based tourism that involves education and interpretation of the natural environment and is managed to be ecologically sustainable.

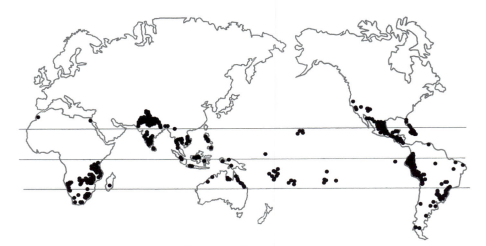

Figure 1.4 Locations of eco-tourist resorts around the world.

This 'nature-based' virtue seems to be a powerful keyword when it comes to developing a resort in a tropical location. Nevertheless, the term 'eco-tourism' all too often appears to be a misnomer and more an idea than an actual practice. As it is popularly understood, eco-tourism is more about watching nature than about staying in tune with it. One advertisement of an 'eco-resort' in northern Australia suggested contact with the environment of a tropical rainforest from luxuriously fitted and obviously extravagant accommodation, with air-conditioning and satellite TV sets in all rooms, imported marble floors in common areas and other such 'enhancements'. This is an absolutely unsustainable approach to eco-tourism, which should be deprecated as unacceptable in this setting.

For the reasons previously indicated, tourism in tropical areas – perhaps more than anywhere else – should contribute to sustainable development and be integrated with the natural, cultural and human environment. It must respect the fragile balances that characterise many tropical destinations, particularly small islands and environmentally sensitive areas such as the coast. Eco-tourism, when mindfully developed, is capable of ensuring an acceptable evolution as regards its influence on natural resources, biodiversity and the capacity for assimilation of any impacts, generated waste, emissions and residues.

From a resort designer/planner's point of view, one of the more significant aspects of eco-tourism is that eco-tourists are encouraged to get involved in primarily, if not exclusively, outdoor activities such as wilderness exploration, water sports, scenic trips or even so-called 'soft' pastimes such as photographic expeditions. This particular focus of eco-tourism determines the character of the visit in the tropics as 'outdoor-oriented'. Thus, tourist facilities and resorts are frequently perceived as merely overnight shelters and a base for these daytime activities. This applies not only to tourists staying in a resort on holiday. Even business meetings and conferences, when organised in a tropical resort, tend to shift the focus of the meeting from plenary sessions to discussions in small 'problem groups' – often moved outdoors. We should expect that this purpose will be reflected in the character of the resort architecture.

1.2
Delineation of the tropics

Definition of what constitutes the tropics can pose a considerable problem. The trouble usually starts with a popular meaning of the term, which often and rather inappropriately refers to only a part of the tropics, namely the 'wet tropics'. For instance, according to a broad classification of climates for building purposes given by Szokolay and Sale (1979), which is a variation of many similar proposals, the tropics are a zone within a group of hot humid climates. Geographical system-based classifications (e.g. Köppen–Geiger–Pohl scheme) are also popular and widely used, and include both humid and arid tropics in the group of tropical climates.

The zone's name originates from the Greek word for 'turning' – the farthermost latitudes where the sun can be observed in the zenith and a point where it 'turns back' in its annual march through the sky. These can vary slightly due to irregularities in the Earth's rotation. In the northern hemisphere the extreme latitude of 23.5 °N is called the Tropic of Cancer, while in the southern hemisphere it is the Tropic of Capricorn at 23.5 °S. Taking the Tropics (the latitudes) as boundaries of the zone, however, would exclude from the 'tropics' (the climatic zone) large areas such as the South California Peninsula and North Mexico or South Africa. The climates of those areas show profiles similar to the regions, which are within the boundaries determined by the latitudes of both tropics.

There are suggestions of dividing the Earth's surface into 'tropical' and 'extra-tropical' halves setting northern and southern boundaries between them at 30° with much the same result. Geographers prefer to define the tropics as that part of the world where atmospheric processes differ decidedly and sufficiently from those in higher latitudes, with seasonally fluctuating lines between easterly and westerly winds in the middle troposphere serving as the boundaries, which is not very helpful from our point of view.

One climate classification suggested calling the 'tropics' all areas where the mean temperature of the coldest month of the year is higher than 18°C (or 65°F), irrespective of their geographical location. This definition, however, excludes areas such as most of Central Australia and a large part of Indochina – located between the Tropics and, in principle, climatically similar to other areas covered by this definition.

Another definition of the tropics includes in the zone such regions where the daily temperature range exceeds the yearly range of daily means. This approach would result in an exclusion of areas such as most of the Arab and Indian peninsulas, and Indochina again.

It seems that using instead a simple criterion of the mean annual temperature, one that is above 20°C, is more practical. Application of this criterion would extend the tropics beyond the 'tropical latitudes' to approx. 35–40°N and 30–35°S, and include almost the entire African continent, southern Asia, large parts of South America and Australia, and the southern USA. This definition could be further refined following a suggestion that areas within the zone where the mean daily temperature on a warm design-day (a day representative of the prevalent conditions taken as the basis for the design) in the warmest month of a year drops below 27°C should be excluded. This generally applies to high altitude regions – more than 1500 metres above sea level. Many of these areas could, perhaps more appropriately, be called 'subtropical'.

In a group of definitions based on human response rather than purely climatic factors, Atkinson (1953) suggested a classification of tropical climates which has been widely accepted and proven useful. The classification is based on only two factors: air temperature and humidity as, seemingly, these two factors dominate human perception of comfort/discomfort in the tropics. Although still not ideal, this classification is generally the most popular and widely accepted one. Based on the effects of variation in the extreme values of temperature and humidity, the tropical regions can be divided into the following three major groups and their three subgroups:

1. Warm–humid equatorial climate.
   1a. Warm–humid island/trade wind climate.
2. Hot–dry desert/semi-desert climate.
   2a. Hot–dry maritime desert climate.
3. Composite/monsoon climate – a combination of climates 1 and 2.
   3a. Tropical upland climate.

It is worth noting that the sea influence has been acknowledged to the extent of arranging 'maritime' climates into separate subgroups, namely 1a and 2a. These 'maritime' or 'coastal' tropics are the focus of this book. They are representative of regions and areas most popular among 'inter-climatic' travellers. These regions and areas are also primary targets for tourist developments.

It is rather obvious that, for use in the built environment, a definition of the tropics based on broad 'geographical' terms of reference is unsatisfactory. The required data inputs are different from variations in temperature and precipitation affecting vegetation. We build to filter and modify various geographical impacts, and the climatic ones in particular. Thus, the definition should refer to the required response by the building to achieve the comfort of its occupants. Following a similar suggestion made by Koenigsberger *et al.* in 1973, the definition of the tropics, adopted also for this publication, is:

> Tropical climates are those where heat is the dominant problem, where for the greater part of the year buildings serve to keep the occupants cool, rather than warm, and where the annual mean temperature is not less than 20°C.

Designers and planners working in tropical locations have to respond to heat, which is a dominant problem throughout extended periods of time, and address a few other climatic factors applicable to a tourist facility's design. Tropical climates are challenging but also offer opportunities. It can be demonstrated that knowledgeable and skilful utilisation of the climate greatly enhances the 'tropical experience' – probably the most sought-after commodity in tropical eco-tourism (Figure 1.5).

1.2.1 Tropical climates and the building

The tropical climate influence is a little different for people and for the buildings they occupy. The elements of climate influencing our comfort are solar radiation, temperature and humidity, as well as availability of wind and breezes to alleviate combined effects of the former three. Buildings in the tropics are also affected by temperature and humidity, but their integrity requires considering wind pressure and precipitation in the first instance.

Tropical climates are those where persistent excessive heat is a dominant problem. Our ability to respond to the heat depends largely on the moisture content in the air. This in turn, because of evaporation, is directly related to precipitation. If a region receives more than 500 mm (or 20 inches) of precipitation annually, there is too much evaporating water to be absorbed by the air and relative humidity increases as a result. Most climates of this type are found within a band 15° north and south of the equator. The American Society of Heating Refrigeration and Air-conditioning Engineers (ASHRAE) has described hot–humid climate as areas characterised by a 67°F (approximately 19.4°C) or higher wet bulb temperature for 3000 or more hours (equivalent of 125 days) during the warmest six consecutive months of the year, or a 73°F (22.8°C) or higher wet bulb temperature for 1500 or more hours during the warmest six consecutive months of the year. Typically, air temperatures in this equatorial band would range between 27 and 32°C (around 80–90°F) during the day

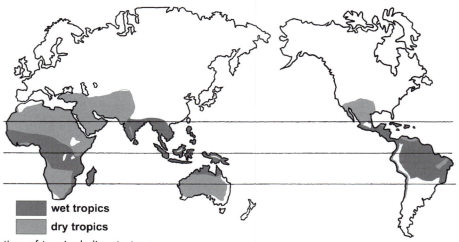

Figure 1.5 Distribution of tropical climate types.

and 21–27°C (around 70–80°F) at night with very little variation throughout the year. Precipitation and relative humidity (RH) are high with RH exceeding 75 per cent for most of the time.

Figure 1.6 illustrates the meteorological data collected at tropical locations around the world and illustrates the type of conditions to be found within the tropics. Annual average of mean daily maximum temperatures in these sample locations ranges from around 24°C in several island locations (Honolulu, Noumea, Fitzroy Island, Tamatave and Port Louis) to 35°C in Bangkok; annual average daily minimum from around 14°C in Broome to nearly 27°C at Minnicoy and in Bombay. Annual rainfall totals display a much larger variety ranging from 71.3 mm in the arid climate of Sao Tomé to 4172 mm in monsoonal Padang, Indonesia. Despite differences, all the listed locations have many shared characteristics and are representative of a great many more locations in the tropics. The following discussion concentrates on extremes rather than on average conditions. Figure 1.7.

One must remember that even within the wet tropics as described above, areas close to the coast

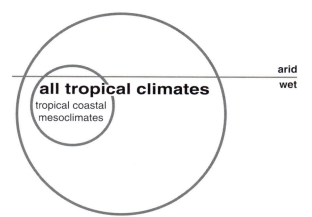

Figure 1.7   Position of the coastal tropics among all tropical climates.

display a few significant differences. The general characteristics of the tropics can be largely modified by a distinctive addition of localised influence of a large body of water. Although the influence of the sea can be felt even several kilometres inland, in many places its impact is limited to only 1–2 km from the shore because of hills or mountain ranges running

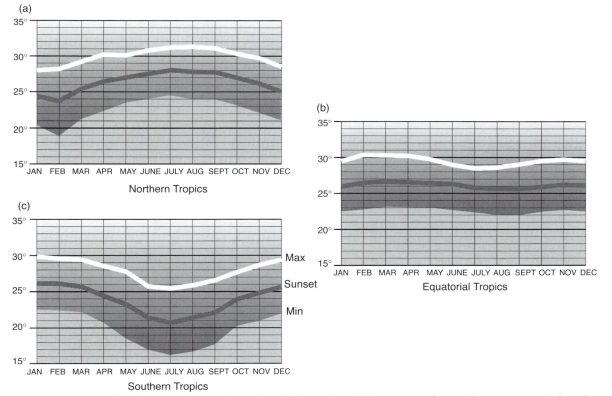

Figure 1.6   Maximum and minimum temperature, humidity and rainfall averages for northern, equatorial and southern tropical locations.

along the coast. However contained, tropical coastal regions are not ideally uniform in terms of their climatic characteristics. This is because site-specific factors form small-scale patterns of microclimates in any given climatic context. Locations within even quite a small area show noticeable topo-climatic differences. The coastal zones demonstrate otherwise relatively few and quite small macro-scale climatic differences in terms of temperature, rainfall, radiation or humidity variation (Figure 1.8).

The climate of a particular site (or microclimate) is a condition linked to, but not strictly derived from, the site location. At least, not to the extent that general inclination to perceive the climate would suggest. At ground level a multitude of minute climates may exist side by side, varying sharply with an elevation difference of only a few metres and within very small horizontal distances. For example, the wind speed, cloudiness, precipitation and humidity conditions are often very different on the windward and on the leeward slopes. These deviations should be analysed and utilised for making the correct siting decisions and microclimate improvements (Figure 1.9).

One has to be careful of comparisons because meteorological data are usually collected by meteo-

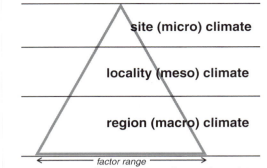

Figure 1.9 Range of climatic conditions found in macro-, meso- and microclimates.

rological stations at airports or airfields and can be distorted – by large masses of concrete runways and/or above-normal exposure to direct solar radiation, which follows deliberate clearing of all taller vegetation. It was Victor Olgyay who noted as early as 1963 that the climate of a particular area or mesoclimate can differ considerably from the regional climate (macroclimate) due to, for example, site topography, continent–sea influences and forestation ratio. Hence, most often, a general climate description is inadequate for building design purposes. Moreover,

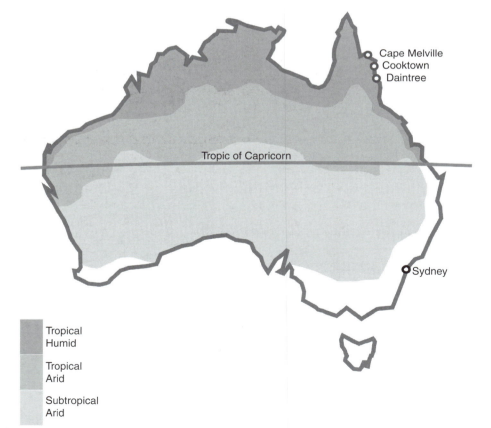

Figure 1.8 Distribution of tropical climatic zones in Australia.

it is necessary, in theory, to collect data for at least 10 years (usually about 30 years) to achieve recordings that have statistical significance. One could even argue that, with weather as variable as that, for instance, in Australia, rainfall records for 150 years and temperature records for 50 years or more may be considered necessary to adequately determine and describe the climate. As this is usually either impracticable or impractical, particularly at times of more rapid climate changes, some care in interpretation of results, when obtained through statistical manipulation of available data, is recommended.

It gets even more complicated and difficult when we move down to an individual building level. A great deal of effort, technical skill and judgement, gained from experience, is usually required to bridge the gap between the raw climatic data and appreciation of its effects on the internal environment created by a particular building design. In many situations, the data one would like to have are not available, while in other cases one is unsure of an appropriate technique to use in evaluating the effects of available data. Climatic influences are particularly evident in so-called 'free-running' or 'passive' buildings, which do not employ air-conditioning devices.

Every eco-resort should aspire to have its indoor environment controlled without support from mechanical means and respond to the climate by virtue of its design only. The aim of such climate-responsive architecture is to provide protection from the negative climatic factors and take advantage of the positive ones in order to meet the comfort requirements of the occupants. It should do this by consuming the minimum amount of energy or no energy at all. Ideally, information on local climate and reliable local experience should be considered jointly to fully appreciate 'positive' and 'negative' climatic influences. Then these influencing factors can be utilised (with or without modification) to assess the microclimate of the site around the building. Changes introduced by a design at this level can provide significant benefits, as opposed to attempts at macroclimate and mesoclimate levels, the latter being generally beyond the designer's influence. This approach, in addition to improving the amenity and extending the utility of outdoor spaces, can help to minimise or even avoid what are often more complex and expensive measures in the design of the building itself.

Furthermore, it is very rare that climatic data for a particular site are readily available. For instance, no detailed information about winds/breezes is collected on a regular basis at more than four or five locations in the whole of Far North Queensland, Australia – an area that takes in more than 2500 kilometres of the coast. Yet, the wind is the most important localised climatic factor in the tropics. From the few places where such data are collected, we know that, generally, one may expect very few calm days in the maritime tropics. Prevailing winds are usually of moderate speeds 1.5–3.0 m/s. During relatively brief cyclone seasons, January to March in the southern hemisphere and July to September in the northern one, very strong winds (with speeds occasionally exceeding 60 m/s) can cause severe damage to buildings and vegetation, and disrupt normal tourist traffic in the area. Along the coast and up to between 2–8 km inland (depending on the topography of the terrain), the prevailing wind patterns are modified by sea–land breezes during the day and, to a lesser extent, by land–sea breezes in the evenings.

It is more than 20 years to date since a fundamental work by Szokolay, *Climatic data and its use in design* (1982), was first published. It offered a method of analysing climatic data for building purposes, which is sophisticated enough to be useful in most instances and simple enough to be performed manually. Nevertheless, with an environmental crisis looming and calls for less reliance on mechanical services to provide comfort in buildings, it is possible to improve a method employed in designing building response to climate. Such attempts have already been made. They suggest taking into account a number of factors not previously considered to improve the method and localise the design input data.

Climatic differences between the coast and its immediate hinterland, within the same zone as identified by geographers, are far greater than variations along the coast and merit distinguishing the 'coastal tropics' as a separate sub-zone for building purposes. It seems quite appropriate to narrow a definition of the tropical coast even further to include only a several-hundred-metres-wide belt adjacent to the seashore. The belt combines features of a tropical climate with a geographical definition of the coast. This approach is justified by early observations, which indicate the rapidity of change in conditions causing thermal stress relative to the distance from the shore in similar areas. Such sharp differences in climatic conditions over very short distances can often be found in areas where mountains are parallel to the coast – even if their height is modest they produce a most profound influence on annual rainfall patterns.

It is suggested that, in order to achieve better accuracy, the mesoclimate or locality climate characteristics, which is the data set usually accessed for design purposes, be modified by two factors applied to every building site: the 'hill factor' and the 'sea factor'

Source	Available volume	Grey water quality
Shower	▯ ▯ ▯ ▯	★ ★ ★ ★ ★ ★
Tub	▯ ▯ ▯	★ ★ ★ ★ ★ ★
Washing machine	▯ ▯ ▯	★ ★ ★ ★
Reverse-osmosis purifier (wastewater)	▯ ▯	★ ★ ★ ★ ★ ★
Wash basin	▯	★ ★ ★ ★
Automatic dishwasher	▯	★
Water softener backwash (softened water)	▯	★
Kitchen sink*	▯ ▯	(★ ★ ★ ★)
Toilet* (water)	▯ ▯	(★ ★ ★ ★ ★)

*Technically, a source of black water, although usable grey water can be obtained under certain conditions

Figure 1.18   Main sources of grey water.

- less energy and chemical use
- groundwater recharge
- plant growth
- reclamation of nutrients
- increased awareness of and sensitivity to natural cycles
- sites not suitable for septic systems, and
- economics.

The main source of grey water is anything that is not connected to the toilet (there are systems that make reclamation of toilet water possible). Main sources of recyclable grey water are shown in Figure 1.18.

Issues involved with water conservation strategies in the tropics and in an eco-tourism setting are largely based on decreasing the amount of water used in an eco-resort. This water can easily be saved (stored water can last much longer) and also used in other parts of the property, such as for watering plants. As water in a remote tropical area can become very valuable, simple methods can be used to minimise wastage. The easiest way of minimising the volume of wastewater being discharged is by reducing water usage in general. All technologies that reduce water use through recycling – instead of discharging it immediately – should also be investigated.

To reduce water consumption, we have to look at the main areas where water is used. The bathroom and laundry are the main points of use, whilst the kitchen and landscaping also require water. Simple water-saving methods can be used, so that reserves in the tanking system are used before resorting to the external supply. Efficient shower and tap heads are an effective way to start. Low-flow fixtures in showers can reduce the flow of water by 50 per cent without affecting the comfort level of the user. Not only does this reduce water consumption but also less water must be heated and thus less energy input is required. Alternatives to the common toilet can also be used. Low-flush toilets or even composting toilets are an effective way to reduce water consumption. The latter requires provision of ample space under the building directly underneath the bathroom to accommodate bulky toilet units.

As for linen washing, this can be done either in an efficient washing machine or outsourced to subcontractors operating in conditions that are more suitable. Landscaping is another big-spender when it comes to water usage. Savings can be achieved by planting drought-resistant native plants rather than imported species and by using drip (if any) irrigation systems. Many plants and associated bacteria can be employed to purify water, rather than use chemicals, either in closed or open systems, such as reed beds.

So, which of these can be applied to the tropical environment? Certainly grey water can be used to serve the surrounding landscape rather than using drinking water. It also adds to the total volume of water generated from within this semi-sustainable environment. The technology, energy needed or difficulty of filtration required to purify the water into something that is potable, however, could make the entire process costing close to the amount needed to receive water from external sources. These sometimes complicated and expensive measures should be reserved only for amounts destined for direct human consumption.

1.3.3 Waste and pollution management

Key recommendations in brief:

- Try to limit waste to what you are able to process on site by adjustments to your resource lines;

- Select materials, construction and demolition technologies to limit amount of waste, emissions, pollution and site contamination at all stages of development and operations;
- Be mindful of waste and pollution caused by construction and maintenance materials' extraction and manufacturing processes in places where they come from;
- Contain pollution at its source rather than deal with its broader effects.

Waste is a material which has, or is believed to have, no further use. While much effort is now directed at using materials more efficiently and at recovering materials from what were previously regarded as waste streams, the waste minimisation and materials recovery industry will still take some time before it matches the scale and sophistication of the energy minimisation industry.

Resorts produce large quantities of waste – solid and liquid – from packaging to food scraps to cleaning and maintenance materials, some of which is toxic. In many cases, this waste is collected in badly designed waste dumps, discarded directly into oceans or rivers, or simply dumped in areas out of sight of guests. In addition to visually degrading a destination, improper waste disposal can lead to water and soil pollution through leaching of contaminants from waste piles. Poorly designed waste dumps can result in fires, odours, flies and ineffective containment of wastes. Uncontrolled disposal of toxic items such as paint cans and batteries can severely contaminate water, air and soil resources, threatening the environment and human health. Even where waste is disposed of legally, landfills have limited capacity, which is a particular problem on small islands.

There are many dangers related to waste and pollution generated in the daily operations of a resort. Excessive or improper use, storage and disposal of various wastes can result in contamination of local environmental resources. Use of pesticides, fertilizers and herbicides for gardening and to control insects can lead to toxic run-off into streams, coastal waters and groundwater. Chemicals used for cleaning guest rooms or in recreational facilities such as swimming pools can contaminate local soil and water supplies, and may pose a potential hazard to human health.

Combustion of conventional fuels is the most significant single cause of environmental pollution. Energy use in resort buildings – for air-conditioning, water heating, artificial lighting and a range of appliances – has the largest share of fuel consumption and resulting environmental pollution. As every kWh of electricity used produces 1 kg of CO_2 emission at the power plant, eliminating the need for air-conditioning, e.g. in just 50 guest units, would be equal to the reduction of the annual CO_2 emission by around 500 tonnes.

An effective waste management programme can reduce waste removal problems and costs. Reuse and recycling of products can also cut operational costs. Effective waste management can enhance a resort's image by limiting visual degradation of the area. The visible effects of waste disposal are the most likely concern mentioned by guests regarding their holiday destinations. Waste can also decrease the quality of tourism resources by affecting marine life or even making the water unsuitable for recreational activities.

Waste deposited around the resort, as well as water and airborne pollution, would ultimately cause irreparable damage to the ecosystems while at the same time diminishing the value of the resource that attracted the resort's guests. The resort's design should therefore provide for safe disposal of waste generated at various phases of its operation. This includes solid and liquid waste coming as:

- construction waste, such as excavation material, building materials and equipment/transportation-related waste;
- waste resulting from the chosen power generation method (e.g. water used for cooling of diesel generators, accidental fuel spills, stored or transported fuel and oil discharges);
- waste related to the chosen transportation mode (e.g. oil and fuel spillage into water or on the ground, and fumes from combustion engines);
- organic waste and wastewater generated in food preparation and dishwashing processes;
- wastewater from the laundry;
- wastewater from bathrooms and toilets;
- other room or consumer waste;
- discarded packaging;
- excess rainwater collected from roofs and paved surfaces (and storm water run-off) around the resort.

Some of the liquid waste (so called 'grey water') and some solid waste (food scraps and other organic matter) can be treated on site. All other waste has to be disposed of by taking it away to approved places where disposal of such waste is relatively safe. The waste management plan developed for the resort should ensure that there is no adverse environmental or amenity effect on the resort site and its surroundings or in the discharge area. It must be remembered that both liquid and solid wastes are capable of contaminating surface and groundwater resources. Therefore, waste disposal and even its processing

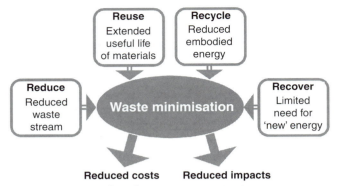

Figure 1.19   Benefits of a waste minimisation programme.

must be carried out in a considerate and responsible manner.

In very much the same way as with energy issues, the principal problem is not how to dispose of waste effectively and efficiently, but how to minimise the amount of waste to be disposed of. Recycling and reusing are among the methods best understood by operators and guests alike and, provided that adequate facilities are available, can lead to significant reductions in waste (Figure 1.19).

1.3.3.1 Reduce–Reuse–Recycle–Replace of waste and pollution management

Waste and pollution management should begin by reviewing the types and quantities of waste produced, and current disposal methods and costs at all stages of the resort's life: from construction, through operation, to demolition. The developed management programme should revolve around the three R's: Reduce, Reuse and Recycle. Only then, the fourth R (Replace) can be added.

Reduce (waste prevention) – means consuming and throwing away less; for example, purchasing durable and long-lasting goods, purchasing products and packaging which are free of toxins, and redesigning products that can be used again after the original use.

Reuse – by repairing items which still can be used; donating the items to staff and local community rather than dumping them; finding new (alternative) uses for the products that have been already used – whenever possible.

Recycle – turn the waste materials into a valuable resource by becoming new products, new materials and fodder for livestock or fertilisers supporting growth in plants.

Waste and pollution are generated at all stages of construction, operation and, eventually, demolition of a resort. At all these stages, effective management

requires that the four-step strategy (Reduce–Reuse–Recycle–Replace) be implemented. Planning and design decisions, which should demonstrate this commitment, are aiming at matching the need with a carefully considered accurate response.

Reducing both energy and materials consumption can be achieved by increasing efficiency (doing more with less) or by doing less. In some circumstances, doing less will be an important part of the experience being sought by clients. Reuse and recycling of materials are well-accepted and useful waste minimisation strategies, which often bring financial benefits.

Waste and pollution management starts at the planning and design stages by reducing the size of a building: optimum use of interior space through careful design will ensure that the overall building size, and resources used in constructing and operating it, are kept to a minimum. Considerate selection of the construction technology will minimise construction-site waste and protect trees and topsoil during works on site. This can be done by, for instance, limiting site works to the assembling of prefabricated elements. Otherwise, all cutting operations to reduce waste and simplify sorting can be centralised, and bins for different types of usable waste set up. Building material use should be optimised: waste is minimised by avoiding structural over-design (using sizes larger than required in given conditions and circumstances) and designing for standard sizes. Careful planning also helps to protect vegetation from unnecessary damage during construction and avoid major changes to the geomorphology of the site. The following strategies can be suggested:

- Designing for future reuse makes the structure last longer as well as adaptable to other uses, and materials and components reusable or recyclable. Because manufacturing is very energy-intensive, a product that lasts longer or requires less maintenance usually saves energy. Durable products also contribute less to our solid waste problems. Incorporate waste recycling into the design.
- Use salvaged building materials and products made from recycled materials when possible and choose building materials with low embodied energy, locally produced if available. Building products made from recycled materials reduce solid waste problems, cut energy consumption in manufacturing and save on natural resource use. A few examples of materials with recycled content are steel, cellulose insulation, reconstituted timber in various forms and recycled plastic. Transportation is costly in both energy use and

pollution generation. Look for locally produced materials (local softwoods or hardwoods, for example) to replace products imported to your area.

- Use detailing that will prevent soil contact and rot. Where possible, use alternatives such as reconstituted timber, engineered timber products and recycled plastic. Take measures to protect workers when cutting and handling pressure-treated wood and never burn scraps because of the toxins contained in them. Look into less toxic termite treatments and keep exposed parts of walls free from obstructions to discourage vermin and insects. Avoid timber products produced from old-growth timber when acceptable alternatives exist. Laminated timbers can be substituted for old-growth solid wood. Minimise use of pressure-treated and old-growth timber, and avoid use of pesticides and other chemicals that may leach into the groundwater, as well as materials that will generate noxious, usually airborne, pollutants.

- Follow recommended practices to minimise potential health hazards. Plan electrical wiring and placement of electrical equipment to minimise electromagnetic field exposure. Design insect-resistant detailing that will require minimal use of pesticides.

- Biodegradable waste is an easier problem to solve. Composting solutions are most appropriate for the eco-resort, bringing additional benefits to the surrounding landscape. Sewage-treatment solids, material retained on sewage-treatment screens, settled solids and biomass sludge can be composted or processed on site. Composting organic wastes such as food scraps, leaves and tree cuttings is a great way to prevent waste. Compost or other organic material can be then used instead of chemical fertilisers. However, composting as well as earthworm farms, leach fields (artificial wetlands) and all other similar technologies requires considering them at planning stages. The space must be set aside and, possibly, cordoned off for sanitary reasons. On the other hand, it is often possible to use fish, geckos, iguanas or other animals to control insects, in place of dangerous pesticides and other chemicals, which does not involve any extra expense. Also, when making landscaping decisions, native plants that require less water, pesticides, fertilisers and herbicides should be chosen over imported species.

- Design room for waste bins in key areas, particularly by the beach and along nature trails. When using services of a disposal contractor, plan for a safe sanitary holding place until waste is picked up.

- For inert waste the processes are quite different. There is potential to reuse some of the construction and demolition waste created by these events. Dirt and cleared trees can be relocated for use in other projects at the resort or elsewhere (some possible uses include flood levies, berms protecting against storm surge waves and roads). In demolition, if done properly, the dismantling of the structure can lead to its reuse in other buildings.

All of the above help to prevent waste build-up on site or in landfill. Recyclable materials do not benefit the immediate environment in the resort, but if initiatives like recycling are implemented it would help to promote the resort's 'green' image.

1.3.4 Impact of building materials and construction technology

Key recommendations in brief:

- Select materials in small modular sizes that do not require heavy machinery to handle;
- Select technologies, either vernacular or prefabricated, with low water requirements;
- Select reusable and recyclable materials with low energy content;
- Select materials that are durable and require minimum maintenance.

Materials used in tropical eco-resort buildings have potentially a number of direct and indirect impacts on the environment, both indoors and outdoors. The direct impacts are the ones where materials interact with the environment, for instance by offgassing or supporting vermin. The indirect impacts manifest themselves through a variety of actions required for the use of particular materials in applicable construction technologies or in their maintenance. Issues that must be considered are:

- available sizes, required components, required finishes, preventing corrosion, etc.;
- prefabrication versus on-site construction (traditional and modern methods);
- waste and pollution (water, air, noise) associated with some technologies;
- health impacts.

Considerations regarding building materials and technologies should include assessment of the following:

- impacts of construction methods on landscape and wildlife;

- source and origin of construction materials;
- available construction technologies appropriate for the selected building materials;
- impacts of resort on visual landscape;
- amount of water required by the selected technology and water conservation methods;
- impacts of construction noise on wildlife;
- amount and type of fuels and chemicals required in construction;
- emissions from equipment;
- drainage techniques used for discharge of construction wastewater;
- use of energy-saving renewable energy equipment and techniques;
- use of transport for various tasks specific to and associated with the given material.

The resort designer should aim at reduction of quantities of materials required before any of the considerations listed above would be contemplated. Then, one may expect that the selected materials will not adversely affect human health, will contribute to operating energy efficiency, will require minimal manufacturing and processing as well as have low embodied energy. They should be durable, require little or no additional finishes and minimal maintenance, and preferably be obtained from renewable resources and harvested in a sustainable manner. Materials that are locally manufactured or reusable, which have been salvaged from demolished structures or have recycled content, and recyclable, should be regarded as better for the environment – in a very broad sense of the word. Possible environmental effects also require that non-recyclable materials can be disposed of safely.

1.3.4.1 Design context

Selection of construction materials is a process that occurs within a larger design context. The design process deals with a broader range and scale of issues, and often offers greater opportunities for reducing environmental impacts than are offered at the level of material selection. Basic schematic design decisions related to building size and form can have major impacts on issues such as energy performance. Deciding which way to orientate a building, and how much glazing will be used, may have a greater effect, over the life of the building, than a decision to use a particular type of insulation material. In applying the recommendations listed above, the particular circumstances of the project in question should be considered. Overall, building impacts will be a function not just of the environmental profile of individual materials, but also of the amount of the material in question. Efforts should be directed towards changes and materials substitutions that will achieve the greatest net improvement.

Equally important as the selection of materials is how those materials are used. It is possible to use the green materials inappropriately and achieve no significant environmental benefit. Over the life of a building, it is likely that savings in operating energy and maintenance will more than compensate for negative impacts associated with the extraction and manufacture of the high embodied energy material.

1.3.4.2 Health effects of building materials

Avoiding negative impacts on the health, safety, and comfort of building users should always be the primary concern in selecting building materials. The majority of them are inert and have few health concerns or are used in locations where they are encapsulated with little direct exposure to building occupants. The principal categories of materials that can potentially affect building users are interior finishes, joinery and furniture. It is important to also consider emissions from, for instance, cleaning agents and other supplies used in maintenance and repairs of resort buildings. The health effects associated with various chemicals can be obtained from a number of web-based resources, including the US Environmental Protection Agency's Office of Pollution Prevention and Toxics.

It is important to evaluate both the quality and overall quantity of materials to be used, and how the use of one material over another can influence indoor air quality. Attention should be directed to the materials with the greatest surface area as well as the materials with the largest concentration of volatile compounds. Material installed in the building in wet form will generally evaporate its excess moisture in the short-term – over several hours or a few days. Dry product emissions are usually much more prolonged, occurring over a period of many months or even years. Certain surfaces can also act as sinks and absorb some of these emissions to be subsequently released over time.

1.3.4.3 Operating energy

The energy consumed to provide heating, cooling, lighting, etc. in buildings is referred to as 'operating energy'. At present, operating energy is by far the most significant component of total building energy. Because of the relatively poor thermal performance standards of most buildings, operating energy offers the greatest potential for achieving reductions in overall energy use. Lifecycle operating energy over a 50-year service life is likely to be more than double the initial embodied energy. Operating energy efficiency is a function of the thermal performance of the building envelope and of the performance characteristics of the heating, cooling and lighting systems. The selection of those systems and of materials, such as insulation, air barriers, and glazing assemblies, is therefore a key component in improving performance and reducing operating energy use. Because of the importance of operating energy, identification of materials and products that contribute to energy efficiency should be one of the primary selection criteria.

Where particular materials or products will significantly improve energy performance, the environmental benefits of reduced energy consumption will, most probably, compensate for the negative impacts associated with the material in question. This is not to suggest that other criteria are of lesser importance. Ideally, materials should both contribute to operating efficiency and also satisfy other green material selection criteria.

1.3.4.4 Embodied energy

In addition to operational energy, a considerable amount of energy in industrial activities is devoted to processing materials and manufacturing products for the construction of buildings. Energy used in these processes, the energy spent on transporting building materials, and energy required during construction, is referred to as the 'embodied energy'. Although operating efficiency is currently the key energy issue in buildings, embodied energy is still important, particularly as materials are replaced and renewed over the full service life of the building. In addition, as operating energy efficiency improves over time, embodied energy will come to represent a more significant portion of total building energy. In highly energy-efficient buildings, embodied energy may ultimately offer greater opportunities for reducing overall energy use.

Embodied energy is the total energy requirement of all activities necessary to produce a material, product, or service, from raw material extraction to delivery of the product to the consumer. The term 'embodied energy' does not imply that the energy is physically present in the material – rather that the energy has been consumed in the various processes involved in its complete life cycle. This 'invisible' energy content can be found in every separate activity or stage of the life cycle in its two forms: as direct and indirect energy input. The latter can be related to the tools and equipment used in production, transportation, construction or maintenance; other materials used in a given manufacturing process, for example solvents; energy required in assembling building parts on site, for example welding or trimming; and many other elements.

Calculating the embodied energy of building materials is a complex and time-consuming process. Arriving at precise energy intensity figures is difficult. Energy intensity will vary, not only from material to material, but also within particular material categories. Differences in manufacturing plant efficiency, distance to markets, and ease of extraction of raw materials, can result in regional differences in the embodied energy of the same material. For example, steel with a large recycled component made in energy-efficient mini-mills requires less than half of the energy required to produce steel from iron ores in conventional plants. Energy intensity – the energy required to produce a unit quantity of material – is dependent on the level of processing and manufacturing required to produce the finished material. Natural materials such as wood and stone require minimal processing and energy inputs when compared with more highly processed materials such as petrochemical products.

In addition to comparing the embodied energy of alternative materials, it is also important to assess the end use of each material and the quantities of the material used in typical applications. For example, manufacturing aluminium is an energy-intensive process when compared with producing concrete. This may suggest that from an environmental perspective concrete is somehow a better material. However the two materials are not equivalent in terms of their use and the volumes used in a typical building will vary significantly. Embodied energy impacts, like other environmental impacts, should be assessed in the context of the use of the material or product in question.

1.3.4.5 Durability

Selecting durable materials is a key strategy in attempting to reduce overall impacts associated with buildings. If construction materials quickly become obsolete, or require such high levels of maintenance that replacement is the only viable option, environmental impacts are multiplied. Even if the material in question is a relatively small component of the initial building, repeated replacement can quickly multiply the overall impacts.

Several studies have been carried out to determine the lifespan of a typical building and its

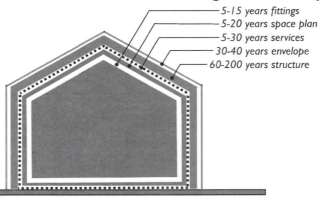

5-15 years fittings
5-20 years space plan
5-30 years services
30-40 years envelope
60-200 years structure

Figure 1.20 Lifespan of various building elements.

components to establish their embodied energy. Because of the way materials and various building parts are combined to create construction assemblies, replacement of one material or component often requires that other materials are also removed and replaced. Insulation, for example, is often damaged when roof membranes are replaced. Durability is also an important criterion in the case of materials that have little or no environmental merit. There are categories of materials, for example roofing membranes, where there are no viable green alternatives and architects must choose between products with few environmental merits. Specifying long-life materials may extend the replacement date to a time in the future when green alternatives will be available.

How long should a sustainable building last? The recommended design service life for resort buildings is between 50 and 100 years. The longer periods are preferable as they reduce embodied energy content per unit of time by spreading it over a larger number of years. When such an approach is not feasible, at least building components should be reused or recycled (Figure 1.20).

1.3.4.6 Reduce–Reuse–Recycle–Replace of building materials and technology selection

Building materials are another area where the 4Rs strategy is particularly applicable. As with the other areas, such as waste management or operational energy, the best way of minimising the impacts from the materials and applicable construction methods required by certain material choices is by reducing the amounts being used. Smaller buildings generally require less timber, steel, glass, stone or concrete. Although the relationship between environmental impacts and building size is not directly linear, in principle a smaller building will have fewer impacts than a larger one.

The idea of reducing environmental impacts by limiting the size of buildings may at first seem to be fundamentally opposed to some principles of standard architectural practice. As a norm, fees are tied directly to construction costs, which are in turn often determined on a cost per area basis. However, work on smaller buildings does not necessarily mean less work or reduced fees for architects. Designing smaller buildings and spaces offers an opportunity to spend more time on design and, if construction budgets are maintained, allows better quality and more durable materials and assemblies to be used. Savings for the client will come through durability, low maintenance and low energy costs.

Another way of demand reduction is by careful selection leading to exclusion of certain choices. In the detailed analysis required to decide on material A over material B, a third option is often overlooked. Can the material be omitted entirely? Particularly in the case of finishing materials, it is worth considering whether the selected finish is necessary at all. Can the floor/wall/ceiling material be exposed or finished in another way? For example, the design of roof assemblies, where insulation is located on the outside of sheathing rather than in the framing space, offers an opportunity to leave the roof structure exposed and omit interior plaster board. In general, reduction of building material quantities leads to reduced impacts at all stages of the material life cycle by diminished consumption of raw material resources, reducing the environmental impacts from product manufacturing and by limiting the quantities ultimately entering the waste stream.

'Reuse' refers to the application of previously used building materials such as those removed from an existing building and incorporated into new construction in essentially their original form. Heavy timbers are commonly removed from buildings before demolition, recut and refinished, and sold as salvaged material for use in new construction. The concept of reuse can also be applied to entire buildings. Where a decision is made to renovate an existing building as an alternative to demolition and new construction, the existing building is essentially being reused. Although some material may be removed and new material added, the majority of the structure is usually retained. One of the case studies presented in Part Four is an example of such an approach. When materials or buildings are reused, the environmental impacts associated with the extraction and manufacture of new materials are avoided. In addition, material that would otherwise become waste is diverted from landfill disposal.

In addition to using salvaged components of the building fabric, architects should consider designing building assemblies to facilitate future reuse of such materials. Building elements should be installed in a manner that allows for their future removal with little or no damage. Bolted connections are preferable to welding structural steel, mechanical fasteners can be used rather than adhesives, and homogeneous materials rather than the composite ones.

'Recycled' typically refers to a building material that is manufactured using recycled content. For example, during the manufacturing process of steel it is common to substitute recycled scrap steel for virgin material coming directly from iron ore. Many construction materials include recycled content. The US Environmental Protection Agency has established guidelines for recommended recycled content for a number of construction materials. A distinction should be made between post-industrial and post-consumer recycled content. It is common in many manufacturing processes to recycle off-cuts and other scrap material. This type of recycling is known as post-industrial recycling and is part of normal efficient manufacturing practices. Greater environmental benefits are achieved, however, through post-consumer recycling, when unwanted items are taken back, after they have ended their useful life, and turned into new materials.

Another consideration in recycling could include efforts to ensure that the substance is recycled into a comparable new product. On one hand, when steel is recycled, scrap steel is used to make new material with essentially the same characteristics as the original one. This form of recycling can occur many times – without changing the original material's quality. Recycling can also result in the production of resources that differ from the original ones. Although this kind of resource recovery can only occur once, such recycled contents represent a lower level of new material use and, in some cases, this can provide justification for the use of products that would otherwise have little tangible environmental benefit.

It is worth noting that, although it is technically feasible to recycle many materials, not all of those that can be recycled undergo any reprocessing procedure. It depends on a number of factors, including ease of separation from the waste stream as well as the existence and location of a recycling facility and, most importantly, the economics of collection and transportation. Reprocessing is most feasible where materials are manufactured locally and where transportation costs are low, or where the materials are sufficiently valuable to make transportation over longer distance a viable option.

1.3.5 Impacts from tourist presence in the area

Key recommendations in brief:

- Concentrate and channel tourist movements through the site;
- Create physical barriers to prevent uncontrollable penetration of the area;
- Develop zones corresponding with environmental responses to various types and extent of impacts;
- Contain impacts at their source with visual, acoustic and other pollution buffers.

Tourism developments can have significant environmental impacts, including the socio-economic ones, on the surrounding inland and coastal areas. The previous sections of this book have addressed some of the actions that designers and developers can take to minimise and/or prevent negative effects from those impacts. Beyond simply reducing the local impacts, resorts can also seek opportunities that benefit biodiversity and nature conservation by improving the state of the environment at a regional or national level. Such actions can be particularly important in countries where capacity and resources for environmental conservation are limited. Conservation of the environment locally can help to preserve tourism resources in a broader perspective.

In many places, and in the tropics probably more so than elsewhere, the natural environment is the principal basis of a holiday. Correct course of action can minimise the risks of future environmental

2.0
A question of comfort

As eco-tourism develops and reaches out to tropical areas, it encounters conditions previously thought of as 'out of comfort limits'. For some time now, with the use of dedicated building systems, we have been able to provide indoor comfort even under the harshest tropical conditions. Nevertheless, air-conditioning cannot be considered an appropriate option for eco-resorts. Furthermore, comfort in the tropics can be achieved also with passive design, which appears to be a viable alternative. Passive means are quite capable of providing comfort levels acceptable to the majority of users of tropical eco-tourist resorts. Indoor climate modification with passive rather than power-supported design also means that comfort is provided in a way that goes hand in hand with the principles of this eco-friendly form of tourism. These issues are presented in more detail in Part Three.

When do we feel comfortable? What kind of environment do we consider to have this desirable quality? 'Comfort' is difficult to define. Hence, it is normally given a negative description as 'a lack of discomfort' or 'a state at which any change would cause discomfort'. Increasing sophistication in environmental engineering has given rise to the notion that it is possible to have an ideal environment, which would provide a condition of 'perfect comfort': a condition where all sources of discomfort are absent. However, there is growing evidence that strict control of comfort parameters does not necessarily contribute to our well-being. Human comfort escapes simplistic or sharp-edged definition. Too many facts indicate a very subjective and contextual nature of this phenomenon. It could be argued that problems of this highly individual nature of comfort/discomfort can be overcome with social survey methods, such as comfort-vote techniques or hybrid methods, which include similar sampling techniques, for instance the Predicted Mean Vote (PMV) or Predicted Percentage Dissatisfied (PPD). Nevertheless, both the various comfort definitions and the values proposed as the representation of this concept cannot be accepted without reservations.

For the following discussion, a new term has to be introduced. A set of favourable conditions will be referred to as environmental comfort. The basic literature of the subject uses for this purpose a concept of thermal comfort, which is only a subset of environmental comfort. Thermal comfort, believed to be a dominant problem in tropical climates, represents acceptable conditions of heat exchange between a human body and its surroundings.

However, a case can be made that for considerations regarding climate-responsive architecture in extreme conditions, it is appropriate to include non-thermal factors, such as lighting and noise levels, as well. One could add smell and touch, which are no less important, and even time – in the form of seasonal and diurnal patterns – as all our senses are stimulated simultaneously. We feel warm or cool at the same time as we hear background noise, see the colour of surfaces, appreciate scents as well as the quality and the quantity of light entering through windows, and are aware of subtle changes in these and other factors while progressing through the day. The need for more inclusive definition is further emphasised once we focus on the environment for leisure. Many environmental conditions that are tolerable at work, domestic chores and other everyday activities can cause serious discomfort during holidays, and the opposite may also be found true.

The variables, having some impact on sensation of comfort, appear in two groups. In the first group, variables are related to the physical environment itself:

- air temperature;
- mean radiant temperature;
- atmospheric humidity;
- relative air velocity;
- light; and
- sound.

There are other contributing climatic factors (precipitation, cloud cover and air purity/turbidity) but they can be merely effects of the variables listed above working in combination with each other.

Variables in the second group represent human factors. They relate to differences between individuals and their behavioural adjustments that may affect perception of the building's indoor environment:

- thermal insulation of clothing;
- activity level (expressed as a corresponding metabolic rate);
- habituation and acclimatisation;
- body constitution (shape, subcutaneous fat);

Figure 2.12   Self-shading of the wall.

reference. Any shading coefficient above 0.2 must be considered too high in the tropics.

In both movable and fixed categories, there are three types of shading devices:

- horizontal, for shading from overhead sun radiation;
- vertical, recommended for shading from radiation falling sideways;
- a combination of both horizontal and vertical (sometimes called 'egg-crate' shades).

The most popular are shades of the first type. They can take the shape of large surface devices, such as awnings, or be designed as divisible screens, for example louvres. Vertical shades can be incorporated into the building structure as 'wing walls' or be used as blade screens, similarly to horizontal shades. Shading devices are often designed so that they can be operated to allow for seasonal or current desirable adjustments. In such cases, vertical louvres, when used at east or west sides of a building, have an advantage over horizontal ones in that they need adjustment less frequently.

Movable shades are better suited to conditions changing in a broad range. They can be most effective in providing the required shading although they can also pose problems of stability (and, as a consequence, safety during the cyclone season) and maintenance. There are few examples of fixed shades that are efficient at controlling the direct component of solar radiation and which, at the same time, permit a view. In the design of fixed shades a design procedure can be used in which the desired ('free') geometric form is compared with calculated (manually or by a computer) vertical and horizontal shadow angles for a given design period. The redundant parts can be then removed, which may result in original and attractive shapes for the shades (Figure 2.15).

Shading can also be provided by vegetation and topography of the site. Neighbouring landforms, structures and vegetation can all be used for this purpose. In the tropics, where overheating is likely throughout most of the year, it is sensible to take advantage of land features and construct the building on a part of the block which is best shaded during the year. To do this, the sun path as well as orientation and tilt of the land must be considered together with exact location and type of vegetation used.

Design aids for sunshading both manual, such as shading protractors, and various computer programs, have been available for many years, however there is no evidence of their widespread use. Likewise, many architectural designs exhibit total disregard for sunshading principles and a purely formal treatment of

location of openings and/or shade the openings exposed to sunshine. Generally, it is recommended that there are no openings in western and eastern walls and that plants do not obstruct the free flow of air over the building envelope (including air movement parallel to the wall surfaces). When windows are protected with shading devices, these are best placed on the outside of the glazed openings, so that they can lose heat absorbed from the sun to the ambient air rather than to the interior (Figure 2.14).

The effectiveness of shading is expressed by the shading coefficient: a ratio of the solar energy passing through a shaded opening to the energy that would pass through the opening if it were unprotected. Usually, a simple window (3 mm float glass) is taken as a

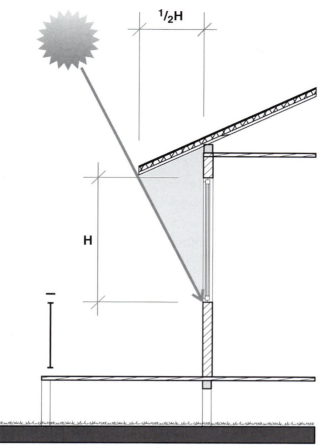

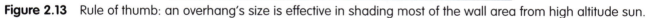

Figure 2.13 Rule of thumb: an overhang's size is effective in shading most of the wall area from high altitude sun.

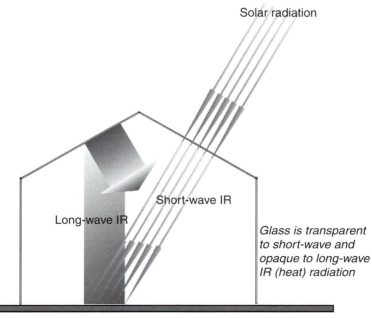

Solar radiation

Short-wave IR

Long-wave IR

Glass is transparent to short-wave and opaque to long-wave IR (heat) radiation

Figure 2.14 The greenhouse effect.

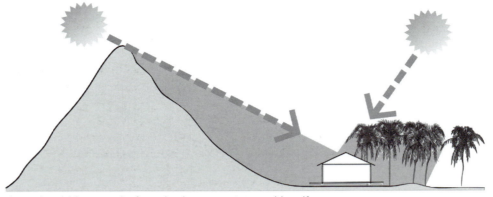

Figure 2.15 Shading should be sought from both vegetation and landforms.

this problem – so important in this climate (Figure 2.16). Sunshades should not be mere ornaments but offer effective protection against solar radiation at all periods when required.

The use of parasol roofs or ventilated roof spaces (attics) is somewhat controversial. Some would argue that the thermal benefit of such a solution does not justify the likely higher cost. As a heat gain prevention strategy, ventilated attics can only prevent convective heat flow from the roof, which is a minor part of a total heat transfer at less than 10 per cent of the total heat flow. Nevertheless, the role of the roof acting as a parasol for the ceiling – especially if the underside has a low-emittance surface (such as 'coolclad'), thus effectively shading a ceiling structure from the impact of solar radiation – cannot be discarded. A carefully designed parasol solution supported with appropriate materials can ensure that such a roof/ceiling assembly will provide internal ceiling temperature at not-higher-than ambient air level. This, in turn, would mean that radiation from the ceiling would not need to be taken into consideration. It would then be sufficient to remove hot air from under the ceiling to appreciably lower the temperature of the top layers of air within the building's volume.

The final aspect of the heat gain minimisation strategy is a consideration given to the material solution. Direct solar radiation increases the temperature of sunlit surfaces. This accelerates the rate at which heat flows into the body of the material. The increase very much depends on the character of the sunlit

Figure 2.16 Ventilated attic.

surface. There are several material solutions to mini-mise solar gains occurring this way. Building materials used in construction of a particular element can either resist heat gain from solar radiation or re-emit it as soon as the sun moves into a position from which further irradiation does not take place. The former are basically materials insulating due to their surface qualities (absorptance/emittance), i.e. providing reflective insulation (see below) of the surfaces exposed to solar radiation. In the latter materials heat storage effects can be utilised: the majority of lightweight materials have very little storing capacity and easily give up any heat stored.

In naturally ventilated tropical buildings, where air temperature differences between outside and inside are low, the heat flow through the fabric is too small to consider thermal insulation as a means of reducing the heat flow. However, even in these conditions, insulating envelope elements can be worthwhile. Such a need must be established using a different criterion. In a heat gain situation, with strong solar radiation, it is the sol–air temperature value that must be used to find the temperature difference. In the sol–air temperature (SAT) concept, the SAT comprises the ambient air temperature value and a value which creates the same thermal effect as the incident radiation in question.

$$SAT = T + (G\alpha/f_o) \qquad (2.4)$$

where T is air temperature; G is global irradiance; α is absorptance; f_o is (outside) surface conductance

Thermal insulation, as a material solution, can take the form of either reflective, resistive or capacitive insulation. The difference between them is that the first two resist heat flow instantly (that is, they insulate) while the third one operates on a time-lag principle, slowing the heat flow down. Thermal insulation is most effective under conditions of steady heat flow, i.e. when the direction of the flow is constant (occurs in one direction) for long periods of time. Thus, in the tropics, it has a bigger importance in the warmer half of the year.

2.1.1.2 Heat loss maximisation

Cooling techniques reliant on mechanical systems require fully enclosed spaces to ensure their efficiency. Some people believe that passively controlled buildings also must be super-insulated. While this might be true in the cool climates of Europe and North America, where energy losses are a major concern for a big part of the year, it does not work this way in hot climates. Preventing heat gains in the wet

tropics would typically mean preventing daytime gains from solar radiation, but ambient air is always a welcome heat sink – particularly at night. Most passive technologies may work reasonably well in an open-to-the-ambient-air environment at no additional operating cost. This way, expensive sealing of the building can be avoided.

Passive cooling techniques can be classified according to various criteria: the nature of the heat sink, heat transfer phenomena, the heat storage period, or the material involved. Cooling action can be direct, i.e. when a heat sink is in direct contact with the building structure and/or the interior air. It can also be indirect, i.e. when the cooling medium (usually air) is cooled first and later transferred, with or without intermediate storage.

Cooling effects are created by the rejection or dissipation of heat already present in the interior. After heat gains have been minimised – as far as practicable – several passive methods employing various cooling mechanisms can be used. They can be considered in four major groups (Figure 2.17):

1. Radiant cooling, especially to the night sky.
2. Evaporative cooling.
3. Storage cooling (usually combined with night convection).
4. Convective cooling, for example resulting from airflows around the building perimeter, cross-ventilation, or the inflow of cool air drawn through subterranean pipes.

Conductive cooling could also be considered, even if its actual physiological effect is limited as it requires that a part of the human body is in physical contact with a cooler surface.

2.1.1.3 Radiant cooling

Radiant cooling can be achieved by radiative heat transfer in two different ways:

- direct cooling by radiant transfer directly from people to cooler interior surfaces;
- indirect cooling by radiant heat transfer between building elements at different temperatures and from the warm air to cooler interior surfaces.

Direct cooling of people by thermal radiation has the great benefit of producing comfort at relatively high indoor air temperatures. This works, however, only if the internal surfaces are cooler than the skin, which is seldom the case in the tropics.

The transfer of heat by radiation occurs between two adjacent bodies at different temperatures. Radiant cooling of buildings utilises the situation when a

Table 2.2   Saturated water vapour pressure at selected temperatures

Temperature (°C)	−40	0	23	28	33	35	37	40
Vapour pressure (kPa)	0.01	0.61	2.81	3.78	5.03	5.62	6.27	7.37

Based on data in RK Macpherson (1980).

Vapour pressure of the saturated air (RH = 100 per cent) at 28°C (3.78 kPa) is roughly the same as that for 50 per cent RH at 40°C (3.69 kPa). The temperature of a freely sweating skin, on the other hand, is approximately 35°C and the vapour pressure of the sweat consequently 5.6 kPa. We should expect that, if other factors such as rate of air movement are held constant, evaporation of sweat will proceed at the same rate in these two (very different) conditions. It appears that the comfort sensation can also be modified because of specific properties of a protein, keratin, of which hair and the outer layers of the skin are composed. Keratin is very sensitive to changes in humidity. It is at least possible that these changes are perceivable and, to some extent, influence our thermoregulatory system.

It is generally believed that for most people comfort limits can be established at 4.14 and 11.63 g/kg, or 4 and 12 g/kg respectively after rounding, of moisture content in the dry air (ASHRAE Standard 55–74). Many experts prefer to assign – as comfort limits – certain values of relative humidity irrespective of the temperature or air movement. Typically, they will be 20–30 per cent as the lower limit and 60–80 per cent RH as the upper comfort limit. Day-to-day observations indicate however that, no matter how defined, humidity is an important consideration only when the air temperature is close to or above the upper limits of thermal comfort.

According to Szokolay (1980), humidity of the atmosphere has little effect on thermal comfort sensation at or near the comfortable temperatures and within the vasomotor regulation zones, unless it is extremely low or extremely high. Givoni (1976) and researchers from Florida Solar Energy Center are also flexible on this point and their expanded comfort zones include conditions existing at very high and very low RH values (close to 100 and 0 per cent) at a broad range of temperatures. They argue that, as long as the air temperature is lower than the skin temperature, evaporation from the skin (and thermal comfort achieved through evaporative cooling) can occur even at very high relative humidity.

Anyway, in all attempts at assigning particular RH values the role of human comfort limits seems to be rather arbitrary. For instance, in Olgyay's chart of schematic bioclimatic index (1963), conditions of 70 per cent RH at 103°F (39.4°C) or 90 per cent RH at 98°F (36.7°C) are defined as unbearable. They may seem unbearable to someone living in moderate climates. The majority of beach-goers would, most probably, disagree. In the tropics, and even in the subtropics, this type of conditions can be experienced without much discomfort throughout summer and possibly good parts of 'spring' and 'autumn', for a good measure. This observation, i.e. experiencing little or no thermal stress related to the above conditions, has been supported by a study on stress from 'heat waves' in a range of locations throughout North America (Lewis, 1993). We may conclude that high humidity can become a problem only when – combined not so much with temperature as with metabolic rate – it intensifies sweating to a point and in such conditions that it cannot evaporate, thus impeding desirable 'fresh' feeling.

Similarly, attempts to link relative humidity averages as 'geographical' limits to human comfort may seem doubtful. For instance, a belief that 40 mm precipitable water vapour isopleth defines the geographic limits of human ability to achieve thermal comfort by purely passive design features in the tropics seems questionable. One should note that the majority of the tropics are located within the 4 cm isopleth. Yet, conditions there stay comfortable for extensive periods of time.

A light-hearted example of human endurance in this respect can be seen on a daily basis and around the world in any Finnish sauna, Turkish *hammam*, Russian *banya*, or Japanese *mushi-buro*. Normal conditions in a sauna are 60–100 per cent RH at 80–110°C. In the others, the conditions are very similar. That seems unbearable even to seasoned inhabitants of the tropics...

2.2
Visual environment control

Key recommendations in brief:

- Provide daylight as a principal means of lighting wherever and whenever possible;
- Use vegetation and external devices for shading;
- Use task lighting rather than general lighting to prevent light pollution;
- Carefully select building form, material types and colours for their visual impacts.

Light and sound are seldom seen as elements of comfort, which is most often understood as thermal comfort. And when a project does include considerations of light and sound, it is usually based on data which have not been gathered in tropical latitudes. We have to see this situation as a big mistake – particularly in relation to light.

Natural light is composed of direct, reflected and diffuse light. The former would be usually called 'sunlight' and the latter two constitute 'daylight'. Diffuse light is received from the sky after it has been scattered by the gases and water droplets in the atmosphere. For daylighting considerations, the sky can be regarded as the integration of an infinite number of light point sources. Daylight is then a function of a solid angle of visible sky. To simplify sunlight calculations, on the other hand, it is assumed that direct light beams are, by the time they reach the Earth, effectively parallel.

Natural light (a continuous spectrum white light) brings out the natural contrast and colour of objects. It is also believed that exposure to natural light can have beneficial psychological effects and is required for maintaining good health. Availability of natural light can make an all-important contribution to energy saving; one could say that in recent years it has been rediscovered as an important energy conservation measure, reducing reliance on electrical lighting. Moreover, it can significantly improve the quality of the visual environment as well as influence general perception of comfort.

In the tropics, there is a tendency to limit admission of daylight – mistaken for sunlight – to the interior. Subsequently, extensive – often overdone – shading results in limited quantities of daylight available in tropical interiors. Differences in light levels, which then follow, can more often than elsewhere cause 'discomfort glare' – the phenomenon of luminances much higher than the average appearing in a field of view. Glare is caused by the introduction of a very intense light source into the visual field. It can be mildly distracting or visually blinding for the person concerned. Whatever its level, it always produces a feeling of discomfort and fatigue.

Glare can be caused directly, indirectly or by reflection. Direct glare occurs when a natural or artificial light source with a high luminance enters directly into the individual's field of view. It can be experienced when light sources are incorrectly placed in the interior, or when the sun or sky is seen through openings either directly or after reflection from an exterior surface. Indirect glare occurs when the luminance level of sunlit walls is too high. And, finally, the reflective glare is caused by specular reflection of sunlight from reflective surfaces located indoors or outdoors.

The ability of the eye to adapt to changes in lighting level and character is very important to lighting design. A rule of thumb is that the eye can easily adjust to the change from bright exterior to an artificially lit room when the drop in luminance (the technical term used in lighting for objective brightness) level between outdoors and indoors does not exceed 100:1. Then it takes about 15 minutes for the eye to adapt, of which the first 90 seconds is required for at least 70 per cent of the adjustment. The figures are determined by the need to adjust not only to a change in brightness level but also to a change in the character of light. In the case of a daylit interior, the eye adaptability is much better as it can cope comfortably with luminance distribution displaying a ratio of 200:1 between the light brightness levels outside and inside.

Colour rendering is also very important for visual comfort. Even if this is less significant, it is probably always tiring to have one or two colours predominate. Colours are identified by photopic vision and the human eye sees them best in daylight. This is yet another reason to ensure daylight availability whenever it is possible.

Sunlight in the tropics, more than anywhere else, is associated with heat generated by solar irradiation. This popular opinion is generally correct, considering that to reach the ground level, solar beams travel a much shorter way through the Earth's atmosphere at low latitudes (close to the equator) than they do at high latitudes. Long-wave radiation (including the so-called 'short infra-red' or 'short IR', which is the actual 'heat carrier') is easier diffused and absorbed by the atmosphere than radiation of shorter wavelengths. Thus, with the same amount of 'sunlight', more of short IR is received in the tropics than in high latitudes. Another unwelcome effect of sunlight is health hazards brought by its UV component. It has been found that solar radiation can cause serious health problems, ranging from skin cancers to irreversible damages to the retina.

In terms of visual comfort, which should be the main determinant of lighting requirements, greatest attention must be paid to lighting that is most appropriate for the activities carried out in a particular space. Visual comfort needs in a guest unit section of a resort would not be significantly different from those in dwellings. Lighting conditions created there should be adaptable to the performed activities, to the time of day and to individual needs. To achieve this, the breakdown of a visual environment into its constituent parts must be carried out and an indication given of how optimum conditions can be created for each part and for different types of activity. These requirements focus on:

- orientation, organisation and geometry of the spaces to be lit;
- location, form and dimensions of the openings through which daylight will pass;
- location and surface properties of interior elements which reflect the daylight and participate in its distribution;
- location, form and dimensions of movable or permanent devices which provide protection from too much light and glare;
- light and thermal characteristics of the glazing materials.

Regarding effects on indoor comfort and environment quality, daylight has a stimulating effect that allows us to fight fatigue and stress. Hence, visual comfort should be closely related to spatial and temporal circumstances.

The amount of energy required for artificial lighting in a conventional building is fairly high; for instance, across Europe it typically represents an almost constant fraction of 35 per cent of total energy costs throughout the year – in spite of climatic differences. Correct daylighting design could not only reduce these costs but also reduce the need for cooling rooms overheated by low-efficiency lighting appliances. Daylight is the most efficient known source of light: its luminous efficacy – even in moderate latitudes – is in excess of 110 lm/W while typical values for efficient fluorescent and LED (light-emitting diode)

lamps are about 50–80 lm/W while incandescent lights do not exceed 40 lm/W. Thus, a given amount of natural light is achieved with no more than a half of the associated total energy input required for operating artificial light sources.

The light distribution in a space should be such that excessive differences in light and shade, which could disturb occupants and prevent them from seeing adequately, are avoided. Sufficient contrast should, however, be retained for the relief of each object to be brought out. Window openings and artificial light sources should be placed in a way that minimises glare. Finally, particular care should be taken in relation to the quality of light to be provided. Both the spectral composition and light constancy should be appropriate for the task to be performed (Figure 2.35).

The need to limit the total environmental impact of the resort, including optimising the use of daylight, should be a primary concern, and use of artificial light should be considered only to complement daylight. It is important to consider both the quantitative and qualitative aspects of light in the building design at its earliest stages. Although the energy aspect dominates daylighting considerations, daylight's influence on human well-being is gaining importance as a design issue. The core performance criterion for daylighting design is to obtain pleasant daylit spaces as often as possible, and for the largest fraction of the building interior. In this respect, the variability of daylight, the quality of its spectral composition, its psychological and health effects on occupants should also be looked at when determining what role it will have in passive control of the indoor environment.

In comparison with artificial lighting, daylighting can be considered a technique with risks. Lighting levels are difficult to predict and can change in one location from very low to uncomfortably high. Reactions to sunlight are equally unpredictable. Affected individuals can react to it as differently as to heat and cold. Interesting psychological effects have been observed in situations where users were in charge of their visual environment. When occupants are given control of their lighting, they often delay switching to artificial light until light levels are very low (often down to 50 lux). This situation demonstrates the principle of tolerance when the natural cause is understood and optional control is available.

Daylighting is also one problem that illustrates how application of design principles valid in moderate latitudes can bring undesirable effects in the tropics. In a standard procedure, computing daylight

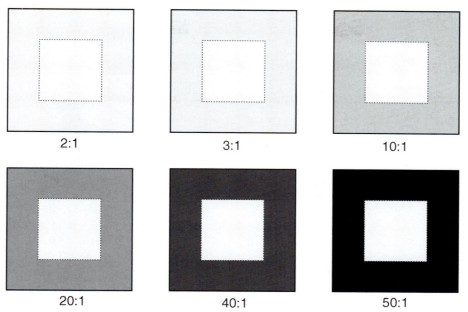

Figure 2.35 Contrast (brightness ratio) can vary from a barely distinguishable value of 2:1 to an unacceptable value of 50:1 which excludes everything else in the field of view.

factor contours is based on an assumption of the CIE (Commission Internationale de l'Eclairage) Standard Overcast Sky. In low latitudes, however, a window providing enough light on an overcast day would typically give too much light in sunny weather. Moreover, designs for overcast skies do not take into account the position of the sun, the time or season variations, and window orientation. These factors in the tropics have primary importance. The CIE International Daylight Measurement Programme is intended to address location differences.

The most general guidelines for daylight control in the tropics are:

- permit view of sky and ground near the horizon only, within ±15°;
- exclude bright ground and outside surfaces of sun-lit louvres or shading devices from the field of view;
- daylight should preferably be reflected from the ground or louvre surfaces onto the ceiling, which itself should be of light colour.

Preventing admission of direct sunlight with the use of shading devices and vegetation can control excessive reflection and glare. Internal shading devices are thought to be more effective at natural light control than most external ones. This, however, contradicts good practice for heat gain control, which should take precedence in this instance (Figure 2.36).

Penetration of solar radiation into a building still contributes to high quality lighting, as long as the sun's rays do not reach the occupants' eyes, either directly or by specular reflection. The problem of penetration of natural light can be controlled in three ways:

- by reducing the incident flux;
- by reducing the amount of contrast in the field of vision; and
- by reducing the luminance of the apertures (i.e., the view through such apertures) as light sources.

Control of direct or reflected sunlight is important to comfort because it reduces glare. It can be achieved either by incorporation of permanent or movable exterior devices into the building design to reduce the view of the sun and bright sectors of the sky, or by using movable interior translucent screens to reduce the luminance of the openings. Reduction of excessive contrasts can be achieved by using light coloured walls and ceilings to give better light distribution. In particular, light coloured finishes should normally be used for walls containing window openings.

In the tropics it is quite possible to exclude direct sun but to make satisfactory use of redirected sunlight: sunlight reflected from the ground and again from the ceiling can provide adequate daylight levels while still reducing solar heat gain. Another approach is to redirect incident (direct) sunlight from the window on to a white ceiling, from which it is further bounced into the interior. If the sunlight can be made to reach the ceiling near the rear of the room, the

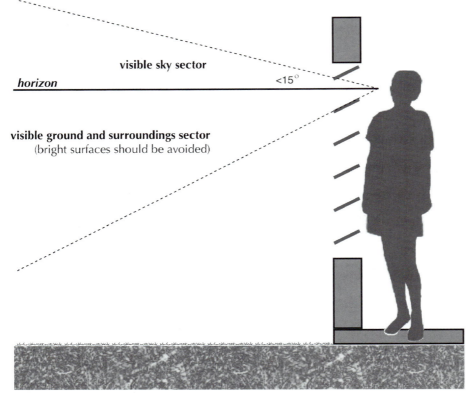

Figure 2.36 Daylighting principles.

reflected light will be received where it is most needed. Most schemes working along these lines propose sunshades or special 'light shelves' covered with some reflective materials and adjusted to redirect incident sunlight towards the rear of the ceiling. Other schemes use special prismatic glazing for that purpose. It is not difficult to provide adequate daylight, often of excellent quality, whenever roof-lighting can be used, which is yet another option.

All radiation, whether visible or not, is ultimately converted to heat when retained within the interior of a building. Because daylight exhibits the highest light efficacy (the ratio of luminance level achieved and total energy radiated) among all light sources, there is some inverse interdependence of daylighting and cooling needs. There is an overall decrease of required cooling when reliance on daylighting increases. This is further enhanced through the related reduction of heat generated by artificial lights.

A key design use of light in a resort is to produce an impression of a cheerful and pleasant environment. This effect can be reinforced by the use of light coloured indoor materials, reduction of indoor partitioning, and appropriate spatial arrangements. Good daylighting design will optimise the collection of nat-

ural light, ensuring its distribution about the building to provide levels appropriate to each activity while avoiding visual discomfort associated with high contrast or glare.

The conflicting requirements of adequate daylighting and preventing solar heat gain have led to the fairly recent development of various forms of transparent insulation such as aerogels, transparent honeycombs and laminar structures. These systems work well in cool climates, but in warm climates their use can cause serious overheating. One of the recent technical advances is the development of special spectrally selective coatings for glazing. For example, low-emittance ('low-e') coatings are transparent in the short-wave (visible) end of the spectrum but their transparency is limited in the long-wave (i.e. infra-red or thermal) end. Low-e coatings are most often used in double-glazed window systems with low-conductance gas filling the cavity to provide added thermal resistance. All these high-tech solutions remain relatively expensive with the cost of a single sheet of low-e or absorbing glass at 30–50 per cent more than conventional glass (Figure 2.37).

The positive effects of natural light on our health have been proven as well as how both an excess of and

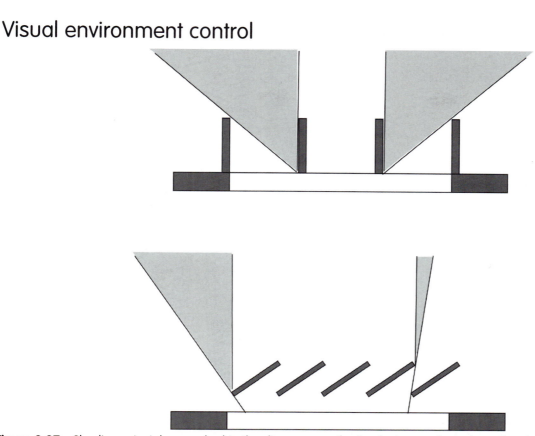

Figure 2.37 Shading principles: marked in the diagram are the 'exclusion angles' where the shade is effective.

being deprived of sunlight affects our psychological condition. Research has shown that 'poor light conditions lead to fatigue of the eyes and brain'. The psychological affects of light reach far beyond the short-term, with 'short, dull days in winter often causing a negative affect on our mood' and lack of sunlight leading to SBS (Sick Building Syndrome). Although artificial lighting can help alleviate these symptoms, it can never fully replace natural lighting.

The requirements for shading devices/light screens include:

- permitting a view of the sky and ground near the horizon only (within ±15°);
- excluding view of bright ground and sunlit louvre surfaces;
- daylight being reflected from the ground and blades up to the ceiling (which should be light in colour).

The major and most commonly used way to filter natural lighting from entering a building is to use screens. Screens can vary from allowing no light through to allowing almost all light through. The purpose of a screen is to filter light and heat to a level that is acceptable and comfortable for the user (Figures 2.38 and 2.39).

Eaves and overhangs are a simple and effective way to shade an opening during the warmer parts of the day. Depending on the size of the overhang, the shadow created can encompass the opening for the entire day or for just a designed period of time. Eaves and overhangs are an efficient way to create shade, and are an easy and affordable addition to the design (Figure 2.40).

Louvres not only work as an effective shading device but in many cases double as an architectural feature. The openness of louvres allows natural ventilation and helps to create an internal–external visual link. Operable louvres suit a wide range of circumstances as they can be manipulated to suit the prevailing conditions: when the sun is low, the louvres can be closed; when it is high, they can be opened. With operable louvres, the user has control of the amount of light entering a room. Louvres come in a wide range of materials, including metal, glass and timber. The many different properties of these materials can be used to advantage: the reflective surface of metal can be used to allow more light into a room, while timber's matt surface will only reflect a small amount of light (Figure 2.41).

Slats are another common form of shading. Vertical or horizontal members break apart direct

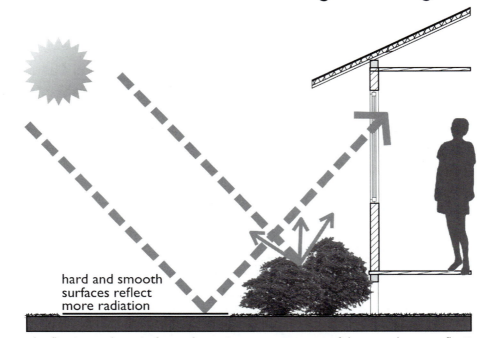

hard and smooth
surfaces reflect
more radiation

Figure 2.38 External reflections: plants in front of openings prevent most of the unwelcome reflections.

sunlight and, depending on the spacing between the slats, can reduce sunlight and glare factors considerably. Timber and metal are the most common materials used and, like louvres, their use can be determined by their properties. Unless widely spaced, slats are not easily seen through, which means they can double as a visual barrier.

Glass alone has almost no effect on light and heat. Light and heat pass through with very little

hindrance. Tinted insulation glass reflects the majority of heat and allows less than half as much through as normal glass: about 87 per cent of heat passes through normal glass, compared with only 42 per cent of tinted insulated glass. A further step up is reflective insulated glass, which only allows about 22 per cent of heat through (Figure 2.42).

Internal and external reflection depends greatly on the surrounds. If reflected off a surface like metal,

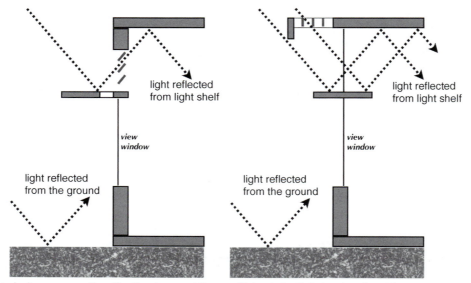

light reflected
from light shelf

*view
window*

light reflected
from the ground

Figure 2.39 Light shelves are quite effective in providing sufficient daylighting levels without associated glare.

Figure 2.40 Prevention of solar heat gains requires not only eaves or overhangs but, preferably, shading the entire building envelope, which can be done with vegetation as well as a 'parasol' roof and double-skin wall systems.

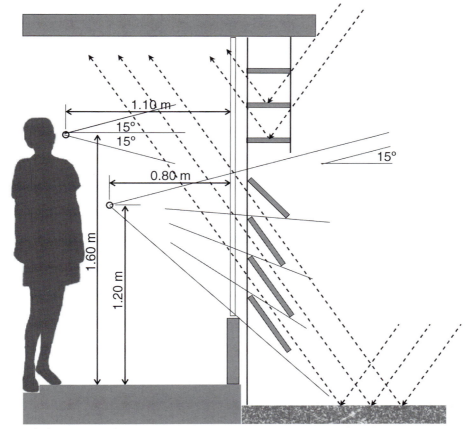

Figure 2.41 Louvres in lighting control.

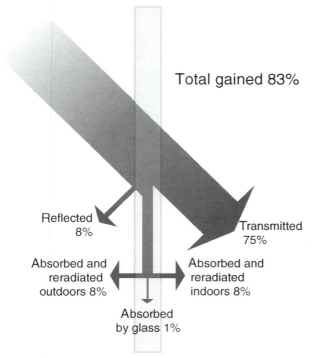

Total gained 83%

Reflected
8%

Transmitted
75%

Absorbed and
reradiated
outdoors 8%

Absorbed and
reradiated
indoors 8%

Absorbed
by glass 1%

Figure 2.42 Heat transfer through ordinary glass.

the light and glare levels can be just as high as direct sunlight. Likewise, lighter coloured surfaces reflect more light than dark and can create an uncomfortable environment. Internal reflection dims the light source (opening) and in most cases disperses it at an acceptable level.

2.2.1 Artificial lighting systems appropriate for a tropical eco-resort

To implement an appropriate lighting system for the eco-resort there must be consideration given to: the size of the area intended to be illumined, the times at which artificial lighting is necessary, and the type of light for the application and the energy used by these systems.

Some strategies to lessen the impact of artificial lighting on the environment are:

- Only install the appropriate number of lights in a room and only use the minimum required luminosity for each globe. This can be achieved by taking into account the luminance level and the radius of the effective operation of each light source. Once this is determined, a suitable lighting diagram can be applied to the space. This removes any excess lighting while ensuring adequate light throughout the buildings.
- Lessen the amount of time that artificial light is used by installing devices such as timed lighting, that switches off after a predetermined amount of time, and light sensors that only turn on when there is insufficient natural light.
- Choose the correct type of lighting for the application. There are currently four major types of lighting systems on the market: incandescent, fluorescent, halogen and light-emitting diodes (known as LEDs). Table 2.3 identifies the amount of energy used by each. A fifth lighting type, the electroluminescent panel, is already in use in specialised applications where soft diffuse light is required, and may find wider acceptance as prices fall.

It is clear from Table 2.3 that the better choice is between fluorescent and LED lighting systems. However, when the times that artificial lighting is to be used in the eco-resort are taken into consideration, it becomes apparent that (with appropriate natural lighting) this would almost certainly be only in the evenings, from around 6pm to midnight, and needed even less in the bedrooms and bathrooms. Considering the relatively short time during which lighting is used, it is slightly more advantageous (cost-effective and energy efficient) to use LEDs. This recommendation has been made because the amount of energy used by a fluorescent tube during its ignition and warm-up phase means that to be energy-efficient the tube must be on for an extended period of time whereas LEDs, even if more expensive to buy, display consistent high performance instantaneously. LEDs also have the advantage of providing a more natural light without the flickering associated with fluorescent tubes, and they have a virtually indefinite lifespan (shortened a little in high ambient temperatures).

Finally, there is also consideration of the aesthetics of what we expect to see as part of the visual environment quality, which is a factor of tremendous importance in the eco-resort setting. Eco-resorts are all about nature and any artificial elements in the surrounding landscape should fade into the unobtrusive background. Powerlines, wind turbines and resort structures should be well hidden from view, preferably using vegetation as visual barriers. Choice of material type and colour should help in blending them with natural elements of the environment.

2.3
Acoustic environment control

Key recommendations in brief:

- Contain sound at its source;
- Introduce functional zoning as a means to control noise;
- Use vegetation and soft surfaces in sound barriers;
- Use masking background sound (ocean waves, rustling leaves) to ensure acoustic privacy.

The importance of the acoustic environment in buildings is often overlooked. Acoustic comfort, however, is as important as thermal or visual comfort since there is a quite apparent significance of the acoustic environment quality in leisure situations. It must be emphasised that the decision whether to use an air-conditioning system or passive control of the indoor climate instead has considerable acoustic implications in a tropical setting. Sound differs from other components of the environment in that it is both a passive and active element of our interactive contact with the surroundings. Furthermore, sound waves are not a part of the electromagnetic spectrum; their origin is purely mechanical and they travel relatively slowly through the air.

Normal sound levels in a resort do not impede its principal functions. Noise levels that could cause nervous tensions or physiological damage are never an issue in this type of environment. The 'sound privacy', however, may become a serious problem. The sounds with information content infringe privacy more than a random noise of the same level. Insufficient acoustic privacy can make occupants annoyed and psychologically stressed. Resort design requirements appear contradictory when, ensuring the privacy of guest rooms, we attempt to provide sufficient number and area of openings for good cross-ventilation. Annoyance or disturbance can appear in a resort environment when sound levels are still relatively low. Such perceptions depend on stimulus quality and information content, duration, past experience, expectancy and number of disturbing events, as well as on personal attributes like physical, emotional and arousal levels.

Responses to a disturbing acoustic stimulus can also vary depending on the activity of the individual and its interaction with other stimuli. For instance, people trying to sleep or relaxing are more concerned and annoyed by intermittent sounds (such as a diesel generator switching on and off) than by continuous or steady ones. A reliable indicator of human response linking all those parameters is yet to be found. The use of either an air-conditioning system or passive controls can have considerable acoustic implications. An operating AC system can generate a lot of noise audible inside the guest unit, outside (near its location), or both. The majority of passive designs rely on ventilated (open) spaces, which allow sound to penetrate easily from the outside into the building and spread from the inside out.

Three methods of determining acceptable sound levels inside buildings are:

- prevention of noise-induced hearing loss;
- ease of speech communication; and
- prevention of noise annoyance, including sleep disturbance.

Of these three methods, only the latter seems to have a practical meaning for resort design. Rest disturbance, caused by low-level noises, can occur without people being aware of it. Studies suggest that people who are unwell may be more sensitive to noise than others. Since many holidaymakers go to resorts to recover from their mental and physical condition at the end of their annual work cycle, they should be put in the category of occupants oversensitive to noise. For this category, acceptable noise levels have been established at fairly low 25–30 dB(A) in bedrooms and at 30–35 dB(A) in living rooms compared to an average domestic situation where 65 dB(A) still feels comfortable.

The primary aspect of the acoustic design in a resort is the control of noise level at the receiver. The sound environment has a temporal aspect similar to the thermal one. It displays distinctive diurnal differences and the control strategies should take this into account. Both the building envelope and landscaping can be used as a filter and a means of control. The required acoustic quality of a building depends on two factors:

- the acoustic environment in which the building is situated; and
- the acoustic design criteria inside the building's various areas.

It is extremely important that designers understand that there is no point in enveloping the building with components displaying high sound reduction quality if there are to be windows or other apertures open for ventilation purposes.

In the external environment of a resort building, there are noises that should be excluded from guest units, such as those from the dining room, entertainment areas and playfields. A logical consequence of the 'design for noise control' is grouping of resort functions with similar requirements. Sometimes sounds which might be otherwise quite acceptable, such as the sound of waves or wildlife, must also be controlled. The appropriate zoning plan can be implemented at the resort level as well as at the guest unit level. Indoors, control of noise applies to sounds from neighbouring units, from corridors or other common spaces, and from lavatories. Effective acoustic environment control depends on the successful separation of functions generating excessive noise from areas requiring lower sound levels.

This can be done in three ways: either by moving the relevant parts away from each other, by introducing sound barriers, or both. Once again the use of vegetation is suggested, this time as a noise filter and barrier, to remedy most of the potential problems. It is equally important not to over-design, i.e. not to specify noise levels that are too low. Over-design requires the building envelope to be considerably more massive than it otherwise would be, and hence more expensive. It can also compromise acoustic privacy. Ultimately, it can negate the possibility of using passive control of the thermal environment.

2.3.1 Noise pollution and effective countermeasures

As the objective of the eco-resort is to be a retreat from the noise and clutter of the city, it is important that each unit is not only visually private but also quiet. A simple way to deal with this is to have the units spread over a large area; however, this disadvantages other environmental considerations such as power, water, construction, etc. For these reasons, it is an advantage for the design as a whole to limit the effects of sound travelling between units and other areas of the resort.

The lower density of people commonly found in a resort situation ensures that there is a greater distance between noise source and listener, resulting in a lesser disturbance when compared to an urban setting.

The management of sound can be broken down into:

- handling of the wanted sounds, i.e. creating environments that favour sounds we want to hear,

usually within a room or building, known as 'room acoustics';
- control of the unwanted sound or noise.

In tropical regions, a great deal of life occurs outdoors, outside the building design and its envelope, making noise more difficult to control. Buildings designed to promote wind flow and cooling, with large openings, offer very little in the way of sound insulation. Sound barriers must be utilised instead to help reduce the spread of noise.

When designing to stop noise, it is easier to separate sound as coming from external and internal sources. Passive solutions for control and protection from external noise in a tropical eco-resort can include:

- Distance: granted this is not ideal in this situation but as much distance as possible should be allowed between units to achieve a 6 dB drop every time the distance is doubled.
- Avoid the openings in the building envelope facing sound sources; this can be as easy as turning the units away from each other and away from the noisier zone in the resort.
- Screening: not in the form of artificial objects but rather with the use of vegetation; this is one of the best sound reduction measures – for such screens to be most efficient they should be as close to the sound source as possible.
- Take advantage of the landscape: use ground shaping (and utilise the natural contours and existing forms of the terrain) to form barriers and break the direct line between the sound source and the potential receiver.
- Zoning: by such location of the parts of the building that are unlikely to be occupied for long, for example bathrooms, storerooms, etc., it becomes possible to use these areas as sound buffers; this approach can be used inside buildings to shield rooms which require such protection, or outside, through site planning, where such rooms can be used to buffer noise from other units and noisy resort areas.
- Avoid creating spaces and using building fabrics that are prone to producing sound reflections; for example, giving plywood a texture or punctuations will diffuse the sound rather then reflect it.

Solutions for control of internal noises generated from within the building include:

- enclosing and isolating the source;
- planning: separating noisy areas and quiet ones or placing neutral areas in between;
- reducing airborne sound transmissions by airtight construction and a noise-insulating envelope.

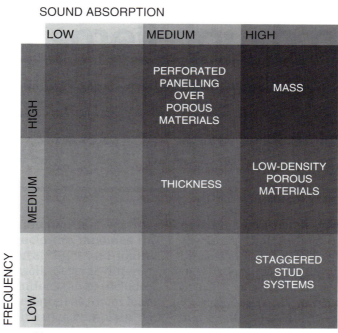

Figure 2.43 Effect of various sound barriers.

Noise within a space can be broken down into its direct and reverberant components. When insulating against noise, both aspects of sound propagation must be considered. Direct noise can be diminished by the use of a screen between the source and the listener, as mentioned earlier. Reverberant noise can be attenuated using absorbent materials. The absorptive ability of different materials is based on the frequency of the noise to be screened out and the mass of the material used in the barrier. Porous absorbers (fibrous or interconnecting cellular plastic forms, etc.), such as loosely packed earth, absorb higher frequencies. Membrane absorbers, such as plywood, absorb the lower frequencies better. Therefore, the material used must be selected to match the frequency of the sound (Figures 2.43 and 2.44).

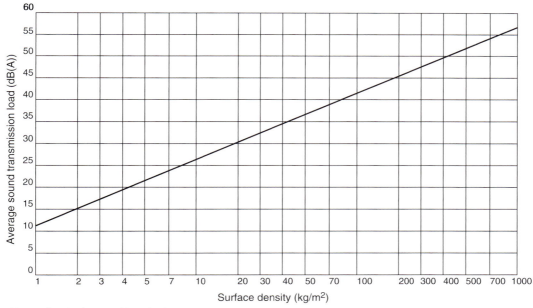

Figure 2.44 'Mass law' of sound insulation.

interpreted as 'one of the more unfortunate aspects of modern global development? As R Punch (1994:6) put it:

> One result [of the revolution in building systems] as far as buildings are concerned has been an almost 'international conspiracy' to impose standards for people and equipment. [...] So that if architecture had a sense of location based on climate, had a sense of tradition based on understanding a way of building, then the new technologies moved new buildings in the opposite direction, i.e. denying architecture any sense of location, denying tradition any sense of continuity, denying materials any sense of place, and above all defying climate with equipment and technology.

On the other hand, nostalgia in architecture is manifesting itself as a fashionable 'return to the roots?, to a large extent poorly researched but in big demand, adding little to the discussion about the way forward. The proper but much more difficult way to achieve progress would be to define precisely the problems, their scientific constraints, their cultural and social backgrounds and respective building traditions, so that the resulting architecture would match the needs of the users. This is not to say that design must be deterministic, as architecture is always about creative design.

3.0
A question of environmental response

Variety and novelty are what people seek in their leisure environments. To satisfy our recreational needs we often feel that we have to go to some other place, one that offers something new and different from our daily experience. For our recreation, we usually leave behind our well-known, standardised and uniform everyday surroundings. In doing this, we pursue other cultures and other climates. Tropical environments have a lot to offer in this respect and are very different from what tourists experience at home. However, while most facets of a tropical holiday are desired and enjoyable, the extremes of the climate can easily become a major concern.

The built environment is usually created to modify the impact of a climate. The extent of this modification can vary. It is recommended that the process of 'climatic filtering' begins outside the shelter: deliberate choice of plant types and landscape elements as well as siting and the juxtaposition with surrounding buildings can maximise potential for shade, wind and other microclimatic changes. Initial design decisions should focus on the siting of the building, its basic form, the arrangement of the space (its functional design), the type of construction and the quality of the indoor environment to be provided. A high quality outcome will depend on the harmony of these elements with each other and with the building's environmental setting.

Although we understand the laws of physics which determine the behaviour of the individual elements of the environment (heat, light and sound) we know very little about the apparent complexity of their behaviour in the building environment situation. Mathematical models used for that purpose contain many simplifying assumptions, which render them too generic except for the very simplest static cases. Moreover, comfort should be perceived dynamically; its parameters vary spatially in a building and appropriate application of this knowledge may be used for necessary modifications. Comfort parameters also vary in time and tend to influence the occupants' perceptions in accord with seasonal and diurnal changes. The latter calls for the users' involvement in provision of comfort. Occupants themselves

may take appropriate action to adjust passive controls to improve indoor conditions more accurately corresponding with their needs.

Why do we need to respond to the environment and how can we go about it? The answers must be given in terms of a holistic integrated design approach and include location, site planning, constructional design, envelope design, building design, materials, functional programme, room design, and operations' management.

The objectives of passive environmental control in tropical coast conditions can be expressed by the following broad strategies:

- to prevent heat gain;
- to maximise heat dissipation;
- to optimise lighting levels;
- to reduce levels of noise and vibration;
- to influence tourists' perceptions of the environment in such a way that local climatic conditions are readily accepted.

In the era before mechanical systems, environmental comfort in the tropics was achieved by means of passive climate control supported by adjustment of behaviour to particular conditions. There are still in place a number of vernacular solutions in regions that represent a variety of tropical climates. Undoubtedly, some of them can be adapted to a tourist resort's environment, emphasising its regionality and enhancing its low energy design. It can be proposed that replacing 'conventional' building design, together with its fossil fuel-powered heating, ventilation and air-conditioning systems, with 'bioclimatic' design is the most appropriate approach. The main feature of the latter design is its passive control of indoor climate. In such buildings, creating rather than breaking links with the building's surroundings forms the indoor environment. As a result, passive design is able to provide an indoor environment quite similar to the conditions found outside. Such conditions, in turn, can be quite adequate for satisfying the needs of leisure travellers to the tropical coast.

Undoubtedly, the major concerns in the design of indoor environments in the tropics are temperature, humidity and air movement; and that is where powered HVAC systems fit in. Air-conditioning removes any need for caring about indoor climate from the catalogue of the architect's responsibilities. Architectural design might appear to developers as a process simple enough to be handled by less qualified (and cheaper) designers or even drafters. That tendency shows its results particularly in the quality of the functional design and the ubiquitous presence of HVAC systems. Alternative attitudes on the part of the designers, rather than alternative technologies, are what is required to solve many of the energy problems in buildings. It appears to be the last moment for the architectural profession to intervene. In terms of energy conservation, architects can again play an important part in determining the energy efficiency of buildings – by designing building enclosures that play a positive role in the creation of the internal environment. What can also be done is to seek inclusion of human adaptability into the practice of climate control.

Architectural design is an indivisible entity which, one could say, is about achieving best performance in all aspects of the 'big three': function, form and structure. Those three components are common assessment criteria for any architectural design. What is different and specific, when referring to architecture in the tropics, is the emphasis on response to climate in order to achieve the best results in any of the three. To design architecture means to design a number of interdependent systems embedded in their surrounding environment. These systems are, in turn, subject to a range of interactions affected by daily and seasonal changes in the outside environment, and by the requirements of occupants, varying in time and space. From this viewpoint, it also appears that architectural design is yet another possible method of energy conservation.

Appearance is frequently the only aspect of any concern to many architects. On a global scale, but more often as a very local issue, some radical views have emerged demanding that aesthetics should give way to energy conservation considerations. It is worthwhile to note that some built-in energy-saving devices, particularly shades, can be employed to obtain aesthetic effects far beyond those available to architects in higher latitudes. This is because shading must be used so extensively. Even otherwise dull and uninteresting architecture can become appealing, lively and vibrant as a result of the play of light and shadows created by the shades. Elements brought by passive design to the buildings cannot only be functionally adequate in performing a specified task but the effect can be creative and 'refreshingly sculptur-

al', resulting in interesting texture on the facades. However, examples of tropical architecture seen around the world demonstrate that there is seldom a satisfying functional dependency which fenestration design for a particular facade shares with orientation.

One has to accept that the natural environment is the primary interest of the visitors to the tropical eco-resort, and that the economic results of a tourist enterprise depend on both consumer satisfaction and the facility's operating costs. It then becomes obvious that architects should apply their skills to making experience of the environment possible and to taking advantage of what the environment offers 'for free', i.e. the sun, breeze and vegetation, to enhance the resort's unique microclimate. It is through the way the building interacts with the environment that architecture of any epoch and locale would normally be perceived, understood and appreciated.

But in a special position that the wilderness areas of the tropics hold for international communities, there are two other very important considerations. Firstly, architecture is there to be a frontline zone, where visitors come into contact with the remnants of this environment, which perhaps also has a world heritage quality. The architecture of tourist facilities, their perimeter and closest surroundings are a space where most of the visitors experience the differences that attracted them to the tropics in the first place. And secondly, it is expected that the location of the resort and the way in which the facility operates will not hinder efforts to preserve what is left of this unique environment.

On the part of designers, the fundamental requirement is a greater understanding of the total nature of the physical environment in buildings, how it is created and, in particular, what role is played by the building enclosure, the system of walls, roofs, floors and windows, manipulated by the architect in creating this environment. Appropriate decisions made by the designer about perimeter elements of the enclosure have a direct influence on the amount of energy consumed by the environmental plant and can completely remove the need for external energy. Clearly, the design of the physical indoor environment is very much an architectural problem and needs to be considered at the earliest stages of the design process.

As stated previously, adequate passive climate control can be achieved by appropriate responses of resort buildings to the local climate. This process of control can be accomplished through thoughtful placement of functions within the resort and its buildings, orientation, landscaping and envelope design. Moreover, passive climate control should correspond with specific needs of the users and exploit the identified differences between tourists, who are only short-term visitors to the tropics, and the (acclimatised) residents. The different requirements apply not only to the volume, shape and functional layout organisation of the building, but there is also a difference between physiological responses. Some early research findings suggest that tourists' attitudes could be the most important factor influencing their perception of comfort. The process of 'psychological acclimatisation' occurs alongside the physiological one, and building design can reinforce both.

Passive design is a viable option for tropical resorts and this has been demonstrated in many places. This can be taken also as proof that biases against tropical conditions might have been built upon experiences derived merely from the use of resorts built to the wrong design. A detailed analysis of user preferences implies that a resort's design should be considered a success when the indoor climate is not significantly more stressful than the outdoor conditions. Such an outcome is achievable with the use of passive means. One might even think that a combined effect of all the features proffered would ensure conditions that are actually better than outside. Improvements may be accomplished in areas of mean radiant temperature (where there may be substantially lower air movement) available even in still weather conditions, light and sound levels – better responding to comfort requirements, and others. There is a widespread belief among researchers that passive climate control is an economically and environmentally justified alternative to mechanical systems.

Architects who would like to influence indoor climate through enclosure design have a broad range of means at their disposal to do so. Their design decisions regarding the building's form, design of envelope elements, materials used, and others can minimise the impact of extreme conditions found outside and the difference between outdoor and indoor conditions. This can be accomplished without input from powered systems. Grouping and separating various functions within a resort can meet some of the specific indoor climate requirements. Varying building volume and/or envelope design in line with different functional requirements can then further enhance the desired outcome. Many means of passive climate control are a heritage brought to modern design theory and practice from vernacular architecture. Hence, their use could bring back the distinctive regional character to the design. Both the quality of architecture and the natural environment would greatly benefit from maintaining this character – wherever there is the local architectural heritage to draw on.

It appears that interest in passive design has already grown into a whole industry. Alternative energy sources are increasingly attractive to the public. Depletion of natural resources and subsequent energy price increases, combined with the economy of scale, could soon result in a significant improvement of economic indicators for those solutions, which are already quite competitive. Economic feasibility lays down a solid foundation on which arguments for implementation of such solutions can be based. What is even more important is that economic benefits of passive systems do not have to be achieved at the expense of the environment.

It seems worthwhile to note that there is probably nothing that shows more variety than individual preferences. On the other hand, there is probably nothing more prone to generalisation than such preferences. Hence, the most important conclusion that can be drawn is that satisfying comfort requirements must be approached with caution. It is not desirable to design for the 'ideal environment'; it is more beneficial to limit extremes, devise simple and visible relationships to the natural climate and provide means for individual occupants to control conditions in their 'personal environments'. The indoor climate should respond to the human need for variety rather than opt for satisfying some sort of uniform and unanimously 'acceptable' conditions, whatever these might be.

Efficiency of the resort design depends on an accurate response to the environment in which it is located. The environmental response should address concerns that are related to both abiotic (climate and topography) and biotic (flora, fauna and human factors) environments.

Efficient resort design starts with careful, well-researched site plan and landscape design, which are vitally important to an environmental response offered and to enhancing features of the site. All facets of the design have to take the environment as a broad context for the tourist development and address its many aspects: physical, social, cultural, historical, legal, and economic, to list a few. All tasks have to be carefully planned and coordinated. This requires a thorough investigation of local conditions, their evaluation, and analysing possible impacts that the development might make. Only then can decisions be made about positioning of buildings and their type, circulation routes, facilities to cater for uses other than accommodation, building materials, technology to be used for construction or, indeed, whether to proceed with the development at all.

A sequential design process, in which dynamic interaction with the environment is being considered long after the building's 'function, form and structure' have been fixed, is also wrong. A product of this process will inevitably deny links with the environment and, consequently, will depend on cooling/heating and lighting devices instead of responding to the changing conditions by virtue of its form and intelligent use of materials. It should be expected that the design context is integrated from the outset and that a designer should respond to the environment; this response will serve as a basis of the human liveability in an expressively aesthetic manner. We prefer to think that passive design, energy conservative design and good design are the same thing.

The design principles discussed in this book can be applied to many projects in various situations. Some of them have been introduced to various building schemes and have proven to operate successfully and without any special problems, benefiting their users. Using these approaches, it is possible to formulate goals for architectural design in the tropical world aiming at short-term visitors. To begin with, it would be meeting actual needs of the users and not the needs that are presumed to be theirs from a perspective of different climate zones or different positions against the investment (the developer versus user 'conflict of interests' should always be resolved in favour of the latter). This involves:

- providing comfort levels acceptable for a significant majority of users;
- offering an environment able to cater for lifestyles compatible with expectations of visitors to the tropics;

- ensuring construction and operation at the lowest possible cost over the entire life of the project, primarily in terms of demand for energy and, subsequently, an impact on the natural environment and facility's operating costs;
- use of passive climate control devices and other means to control indoor climate, such as landscaping and building layout, in an aesthetically pleasing manner;
- satisfying not only requirements of indoor environmental comfort, but safety and privacy as well as functional and structural integrity.

Some of the above objectives can prove very difficult to accomplish but the effort should be made because climatic responsiveness ensures health and sustainability at low cost. Also, central to appreciating architecture on the tropical coast is how it fits the climate and how it takes advantage of the sun, wind, and vegetation. This can be done only if particular needs of the users are assessed and satisfied.

The indoor environment is created by a large number of building elements interacting in a rather complex manner. From a physical processes standpoint, a building and its environmental control systems are a microcosm of complexity, where the only independent variables are the space and time dimensions. All other parameters are dependent variables and so each must be considered in relation to the others. This means that the fabric conduction processes, air movements and short-wave flux injections, for example, must all be treated in a simultaneous and time-dependent manner.

3.1
Location

Key recommendations in brief:

- Analyse climate factors including sunlight, temperature, precipitation/humidity and winds;
- Avoid locations that have a history of unstable weather conditions;
- The selected location should have potential for good all-weather access;
- Preferable locations should offer a variety of local resources from supportive communities, through some building materials, to food and water.

Many tropical areas yield to recent trends and open up to tourist developments. Many such 'new areas' lack access and infrastructure and are not very attractive to local dwellers. A good example of this can be seen in northern Australia. The number, character and variety of coastal environments in the region can be illustrated with a sample taken between Kennedy Bay (lat. 18°00'S) and Donovan Point (lat. 16°00'S).

In this part of the coast there are 34 islands and islets close to the continent. Most of Great Barrier Reef islands are small (with an area less than 4 hectares) and lack suitable landing places and fresh water. They differ in size, geological origin, appearance, vegetation cover, soils, available water sources and a great many other aspects. Distances between some of them and the continent are very small; in several cases the distances do not exceed 1 km but this is enough to deny them a bridge connection. For most of the year, they are infested by sandflies and mosquitoes. Given the difficulties, it is not surprising that until 1956 all island resorts closed for the humid summer months. And yet now, there are several all-year island resorts operating in the area and a number of others are to be developed. Tourist developments bring with them opportunities, which attract residential interest and other uses.

The choice of location is an aspect of a design endeavour that architects normally would not be able to influence. Nevertheless, it is this kind of decision which must be thoroughly analysed. Each location has unique abiotic (topography and climate) and biotic (flora and fauna) characteristics. Most notable in the tropics is the climatic factor. The location climate, both outdoors and indoors, will be perceived though the subjective filter of the visitor's attitude. In comfort considerations, the importance of psychological factors influencing perceptions of the environment is greater than elsewhere. Nevertheless, even the most expansive tolerance limits do not cover all conditions. The bioclimatic strategies hence should be employed to improve building performance and remove or limit the need to provide comfort with mechanical devices.

The designer should have a better understanding of the microclimate and this, in turn, requires a method to extrapolate its characteristics from regional data. A relationship between the external climate, as presented through available climatic data, and indoor requirements should be developed into various measures to prevent overheating, induce cooling effects, reinforce airflows, and prevent excessive light and noise with the aim of improving the environment–building interaction.

The location climate is the averaged (over a relatively large area and for extensive periods of time) weather condition derived from data collected at one or more stations. It describes the condition that prevails in that location. Hence, choice of a location for the development, from a climatic point of view, determines only the general climatic characteristics. The tropics have been subdivided, based on climatic factors, for several different purposes: local government, regional development, weather forecasting, or tourism administration. In several tropical countries, climatic zoning has been suggested to enable preparation of guidelines for response to the climate through the building design.

It appears, however, that the zones, based on climate-only characteristics, can only be used as very general guidelines for the building design response recommended in local conditions. Small island locations in particular have been largely overlooked in this respect and the description of climatic conditions in these places is based mostly on a mere extrapolation of data from meteorological stations hundreds of kilometres away. Islands should be considered individually since their microclimates are shaped by the sea rather than by the land, with all the consequences of this fact; for instance, wind incidence is higher and it can come unimpeded from any direction. Although annual average humidity in island locations is high, in summer it is usually lower than at corresponding land locations, and the temperature range is moderated by the masses of surrounding water.

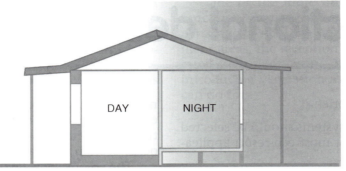

Figure 3.10   Section showing the principle of a hybrid structure.

lightweight structure. The concept has undergone very limited testing in practical situations and remains largely a theoretical conjecture. Nevertheless, the hybrid alternative could prove to be the most appropriate solution for eco-resorts in the coastal tropics.

In the case of some resort buildings, however, it does not seem necessary to use this type of structure. A number of behavioural differences between residents and visitors to the tropical coast make it possible to consider only a part of a resort as the one crucial to the tourists' perception of comfort. As we have argued, it is the part designated for night-time use, i.e. the guest units. Constructional design of other buildings should give priority to limitation of the impact that the buildings and associated construction processes make on the environment. From this point of view, lightweight structures seem to be a better option than heavy ones by a large margin.

Builders themselves can move elements of a lightweight structure and, because of this, the need for lifting equipment is usually substantially reduced. Furthermore, these elements can be brought to the site using all means of transportation including burden animals – there is no need for roads or cranes. Most technologies used in lightweight structures do not require powered machinery or tools, which results in less environmental impact during the construction stages. Having been traditionally used in vernacular tropical buildings, these technologies, more often than the heavyweight ones, can draw on locally available materials and utilise locally available building skills. Flow-on benefits include low embodied energy and less undesirable socio-economic impacts. Finally, yet importantly, lightweight structures can be removed leaving almost no trace behind – a feat not as easily achievable with heavyweight ones.

3.4
Building design

The building envelope – a system of roofs, walls with all openings, and floors both on the ground and suspended – is the ultimate barrier between the indoors and the world outside. The barrier works like a filter, employing building fabric and various design features.

In a hot and humid climate, there appear to be only two considerable ameliorating effects achievable with the help of purely passive climate control. They are:

- reduction in the amount of total radiation; and
- increase of airflow.

Other effects, such as supply of cool air and dehumidification, are difficult to achieve without some support from powered devices and would probably require conscious cooperation on the part of the occupants. This, in turn, would require some sort of preparatory measures, such as instruction and training. Thus, an attempt to achieve such effects is seemingly impractical in a tourist resort. There are also psychological consequences (see Section 2.4) of certain design solutions, which also could be employed. However, these solutions appear to be largely past experience/culture-dependent and require much more research before conclusive results, leading to their practical implementation, can be expected.

Let us pause for a moment and consider the actual magnitude of the design task. A brief developed on a basis of climatic recommendations alone would become, most probably, a document full of mutually exclusive demands. For instance, in order to reduce roof area and solar irradiation and to increase exposure to sea breezes, it would be advisable to build multi-storey buildings. However, this is contradictory to the resort character and, quite obviously, invasive to the landscape. Moreover, high-rise buildings demand, on average, more energy than any others, present a more difficult-to-control acoustic environment, are much more expensive in difficult foundation conditions so frequently found on the tropical coast, and are more intrusive (to say the least) in environmental terms.

A compromise solution would be to accommodate tourist resorts in buildings of a few storeys. Guest bedrooms could be located upstairs while rooms requiring more defined thermal control during the daytime could be moved downstairs. The upper parts of the resort buildings should preferably be lightweight structures designed to prevent any considerable heat gains. Such a solution could be problematic when looked at from another angle: cyclonic winds occurring in the tropics during the summer season can cause extensive damage to light structures and endanger their occupants. Other examples such as better daylighting, achieved by increasing the size of windows, in most instances will increase heat gains. Larger windows, on one hand, will increase intrusion of external noise but, on the other hand, provide psychologically beneficial visual contact with the outside. Noise in the background is undesirable in itself but potentially useful to aid speech privacy as a masking sound. Sunshades would control the period of solar irradiation but reduce the level of available daylight. This list of contradictions could be extended.

V. Olgyay (1963) carried out studies for optimum building shape for a range of climatic zones. For hot–humid zones he recommended rectangular building shape with the short to long wall aspect ratio of 1:1.7. This recommendation applies, however, primarily to dwellings as it improves their overall day–night performance. Resort performance emphasis is on the night-time, and the ability to dissipate heat (by means of effective cross-ventilation easiest available in narrow, spread-out buildings) is, perhaps, more important than preventing heat gains. Notwithstanding, exposure of eastern and western walls to the sun should be minimised and the building elongated to catch prevailing winds and to aid cross-ventilation.

A catalogue of means available to architectural designers is presented in this section. Some of these means could greatly influence the indoor climate of a resort. In the given conditions, some may only produce marginal changes and others would make no measurable impact. However the range of available means seems to be large enough to select the ones, in most locations, that will control parameters of the indoor environment to a desired extent.

3.4.1 Building layout

Key recommendations in brief:

- Promote air movement through narrow single-bank layout;

- Open the plan and design free of interior obstructions in both horizontal and vertical planes;
- Open the building up by providing ample openings;
- Designate open-to-air (without walls) spaces for dining, entertainment and (alternative) sleeping.

For all types of buildings within the resort, one of the most important design factors is provision of considerable air movement. Air movement is considered the only effective way of ameliorating thermal conditions in warm and humid climates. Hence, both the internal plan and envelope characteristics should provide for numerous effective air paths through the interior. The rate and volume of cross-ventilation airflows through building interiors as a result of plan/section design has not been well researched but some general advice in this regard can be put forward.

To ensure adequate airflows, buildings should be narrow and rooms should be lined up ('single-bank' layout) or branched-out rather than double-sided or clustered as the economics of internal communication would stipulate. Some of the spaces, like the dining area, can be designed as rooms without walls. Even if privacy requirements discourage true openness of the plan in resorts, which consist of a large number of relatively small spaces, the design should offer as much area open to the external environment as possible. For example, it is advisable that access to secure outdoor areas (such as on a flat roof) is provided from bedrooms. Such spaces could then be used as alternative open-sky night-time sleeping areas or for day ('siesta') rest. The problem to be resolved in this arrangement would be to provide adequate water drainage from such roofs during the rainy season. A safe removable shade would also help to control heat gains; large balconies are also an option (Figure 3.11).

Openings should be ample as the volume of air flowing through the building is correlated with its size and, to a lesser extent, with its shape. The size of an opening (and the height of its sill, if any) on a windward side should promote air movement at body height, while even bigger openings should be provid-

ed in a leeward wall. In the case of guest units, used mostly at night, the 'windward' side on the coast would be an 'inland' side – because of the direction of night breezes. Breezes coming from the sea in the evening are also beneficial in dissipating daytime heat build-ups that, in turn, makes openings in the 'sea-ward' side of the building important.

Moreover, a slight change of the air current direction between inlet and outlet, both in plan and in section, is beneficial for a distribution of airflows. This way the air flowing through the guest unit moves through the largest part of its volume and reaches into what otherwise would become pockets of 'dead air'. Further improvement would result from using louvre type windows, which can be made to open downwards (on the room side) to 10° below the horizontal position. It is also helpful to install warm air exhausts from under the ceiling or, better still, create a stack effect to allow for vertical convective air movement as well.

Some resort functions can be moved to spaces which are open to the air. The overall strategy in this respect should be to maximise the number of such rooms. This principle applies not only to the resort functions producing high metabolic rates in participants, such as physical recreation and entertainment, but also to functions where activities are moderately demanding, such as dining. With sufficient effort, a solution to the problem of providing secure and private sleep-outs for guests can also be found. In most situations, removable fly-screens would have to be installed to provide protection against mosquitoes and sandflies (Figure 3.12 and Figure 3.13a–c).

3.4.2 Envelope design

Key recommendations in brief:

- Consider the roof as the most important part of the envelope, requiring all 'climatic defences' available;

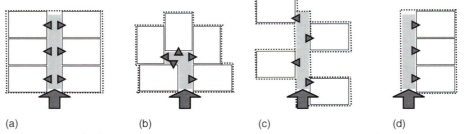

(a)   (b)   (c)   (d)

Figure 3.11   Building layouts: a. double-sided, b. clustered, c. branched-out, d. single-bank.

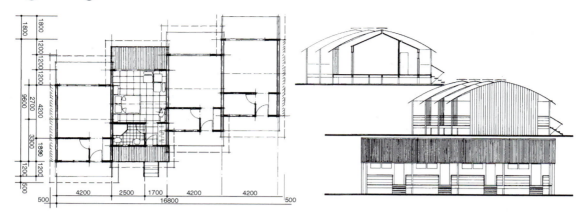

Figure 3.12 Theoretical set of four guest units incorporating some of the recommended features (parasol roof, ridge vents, raised floor, entire eastern and western wall shades): plan, section and elevations.

- Open the envelope to provide relatively free airflow through the building;
- Provide shade to east and west walls and avoid openings in these walls;
- Raise buildings above ground level to take advantage of airflow under the floor and over cool ground/sea.

At the functional level, the building envelope separates the building interior from the external environment and, in conjunction with building services, maintains desirable internal conditions. The design of the envelope and, in particular, the selection of insulation and air barrier materials can have a major impact on energy expenditure and operational performance of the building. Thermal insulation of the envelope is particularly important in air-conditioned buildings. It minimises conductive heat flows and can significantly reduce energy consumed in cooling or heating the building. Similarly, an effective air infiltration control will reduce heat flows as a result of excessive air leakage through the envelope.

Over the life of a building the environmental benefits of these savings in operating energy will, probably, more than compensate for any negative impacts associated with the embodied energy of the insulation. Materials used in envelope assemblies are subject to significant daily swings in temperature and vapour pressure and – in the case of air-conditioned interiors – to large gradients in these indices. The cladding, being affected by the external environment, is exposed to many forces that can degrade building materials. Durability becomes a major issue

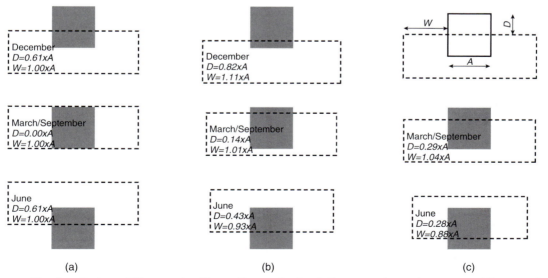

(a)   (b)   (c)

Figure 3.13a–c Shading that would be required to continuously shade the area shown in grey: a. at the equator; b. at 8°N; c. at 16°N (Brown and DeKay, 2001).

as lifecycle environmental impacts are increased if frequent replacement of cladding materials is necessary.

The following envelope design guidelines are aimed at the resort guest units. It should be understood that they are different from other resort buildings as they serve a different functional purpose. The crucial differentiating factor appears to be the time of use. The unit's environmental performance is the result of the interaction of its envelope components, for the most part, with the night-time environment. Nevertheless, a unit's daytime performance cannot be simply disregarded as heat build-ups during this part of the diurnal cycle substantially contribute to its overall thermal profile.

3.4.2.1 Roofs

In the tropics, roofs receive more solar radiation than any other surface of the building. The significance of solar heat gain through the roof increases with the roof area to building volume ratio. If possible, the roof should be shaded by high-branched trees and have a white or other high-emittance finish. The design of the roof is of the greatest importance for keeping indoor temperatures at a not-higher-than-outdoors level. Some solutions will perform in given conditions better than others. For instance, in predominantly high daytime temperatures, an uninsulated double-shell envelope, also known as the 'parasol' roof, can function well. The outer skin shades the cavity, keeping the temperature of the air contained lower, and subsequently reduces the temperature of the inner skin. Ridge outlets should be provided for 'ridge effect' ventilation. Due to lack of insulation, night-time heat transfer from the interior into the cavity promotes cooling. There exist vernacular examples of 'parasol' roofs, almost detached, which perform well in hot conditions. Such a 'shaded' roof system can cut total heat gains through the envelope by several per cent. The addition of even a very thin sheet ceiling impacts dramatically on the thermal performance of the roof system. The underside of the roof and the topside of the ceiling, in such a case, should be reflective to minimise both emission and absorption (Figures 3.14–3.19).

Some research indicates that the thermal performance of the roof in hot climates might depend more on its surface colour and other properties than on its insulation (Givoni, 1994; see also Section 3.4.3). This is a contested issue that requires more research before a recommendation can be made. Nevertheless, it seems that a combination of a high-emittance (i.e. fairly reflective) surface and insulation could be a safe compromise (Figure 3.20).

Because of the danger from cyclones occurring in the tropics during the summer season, it is necessary to ensure adequate structural integrity, particularly to

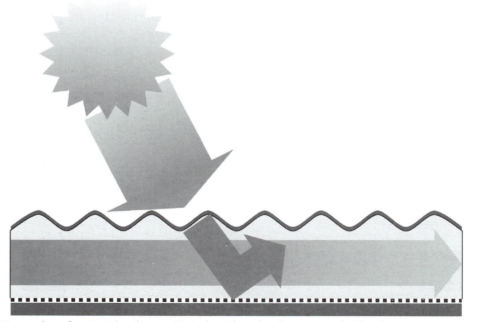

Figure 3.14 The 'Parasol roof' principle: the ventilated void under the external skin stays at a temperature close to the ambient temperature; placing reflective insulation on the internal skin greatly reduces gains from the radiative heat flow.

Figure 3.15 A parasol roof can be used in night ventilation.

uplift. Normally, it would be expected that the roof has an even and smooth surface, and that all elements subjected to increased (positive or negative) pressures, such as eaves, porches and verandas, are appropriately tied down.

3.4.2.2 Walls

Wall structure in the humid tropics has less thermal importance than in any other climatic region. This is because heat flows through this part of the envelope are diminished by small diurnal swings of temperatures. In a resort, walls are used primarily to ensure the privacy and safety of occupants, and for screening from insects and animals. Their thermal qualities should make it possible that night-time drops in temperature are followed by their (wall) cooling without significant delays and to prevent morning condensation. Expansive wall areas enhance night cooling, although increasing the envelope's surface as a means of improving its overall thermal performance is questionable because of unavoidable heat during the day. Shading the entire east, and especially the west, walls is definitely beneficial as it helps to avoid morning and afternoon heat gains. These walls (and any openings in them) are most effectively shaded by fixed 'egg-crate' devices where vertical fins are turned 45° towards the equator (i.e. South-East

Figure 3.16 A parasol roof on a guest unit at Amanwana Resort, Indonesia.

(at which point it would become a sensible heat radiator), and preferably less, to arrive at no more than a 1 K increment at the ceiling. The insulation required to achieve this would have to perform at R2.7–3 levels.

3.4.3.3 Capacitive insulation

The 'thermal mass' effect is produced by envelope elements of considerable thermal capacity; such elements are referred to as 'capacitive insulation'. Although there is no direct relationship between the resistivity (or conductivity) and the density of a material, dense materials tend to have low resistivity values, hence low insulative properties. However, they can be used for insulation in a different way. Thermal capacity is a product of specific heat capacity (heat stored in a unit volume per degree of temperature rise) and the density of the given material. For example, the storage capacity of masonry ranges from 0.204 kWh/m³ K for cellular concrete to 0.784 kWh/m³ K for heavyweight concrete. Most liquids show considerable thermal capacities. For instance, water, which has the highest thermal capacity, can store 1.157 kWh/m³ K at 20°C.

The thermal capacity of building elements having n different components may be calculated from the following equation:

$$C = \sum m_n c_n = \sum \rho_n V_n c_n \qquad (3.5)$$

where C is thermal capacity [Wh/m³K]; m_n is mass of 'n' component of a building element [kg]; c_n is specific heat capacity of 'n' component [Wh/kgK]; ρ_n is density of 'n' component [kg/m³]; V_n is the 'n' element's volume [m³].

Capacitive insulation can be employed as materials of two different types. With traditional materials such as concrete and brick, the storage process makes use of sensible heat, that is, heat that can be measured as it results in an increase in temperature. Phase-change materials, on the other hand, make use of the latent heat of fusion, i.e. the heat required to change the state of the material from a solid to a liquid without a change in temperature. In the construction field, it is usual to choose a material which changes phase at a temperature somewhere between 2° and 50°C (normally around 27°C). Very large quantities of heat (typically 38–105 kWh/m³, i.e. up to 15 times more than for masonry) can be stored when the phase-change occurs. Therefore, a much smaller volume is required for phase-change storage than for conventional storage.

New materials are currently being developed which change their molecular structure without changing state. This transformation also uses latent heat and can therefore be used to store heat. The advantage of the new materials over phase-change materials is that they remain solid. Currently, however, they are expensive, not very reliable, and can only be used over a limited number of charge–discharge cycles.

3.4.3.4 Materials reducing humidity

Thermal comfort is, in principle, a combination of temperature and humidity factors. Thus, in the wet tropics, improvement of the thermal comfort will follow a decrease of either. Some form of dehumidification could limit the need for a high ventilation rate. This, in turn, would allow for use of storage cooling. Dehumidification methods that can be implemented in hot humid climates fit in two broad categories. The methods in the first category depend on the use of desiccants: either solid phase absorbents or adsorbents, or hydrophilic solutions. Dehumidification techniques belonging in the second category make use of various environmental 'humidity sinks', in particular ones that are ground coupled. The use of environmental sinks for dehumidification is most effective when the underground annual average temperature is below 20°C. At higher ground temperatures this natural latent cooling method can still be applied but must be complemented by the use of desiccants.

Dehumidification is usually considered a mechanical process in all its aspects and phases, although there are a few experimental passive methods using desiccants. Desiccants are materials which absorb moisture from the air. They do this either by the process of adsorption, where water molecules are attracted to the surface of the material, or absorption, where moisture is attracted by a desiccant to dissolve chemically.

Desiccants in passive systems are exposed to the controlled space at night and left to dry out in the sun during the day. Interesting results were reported about experiments carried out with wool as the desiccant. Apparently, wool is so far the only known material which does not display significant deterioration of its hygroscopic properties with use. While the results were quite promising, the current large fluctuations in this commodity market make pricing difficult, so estimating the cost of this solution and performing a sound feasibility analysis have yet to be done. Other materials such as silica gel, activated alumina, calcium chloride and lithium chloride have a short active life and show significant deterioration

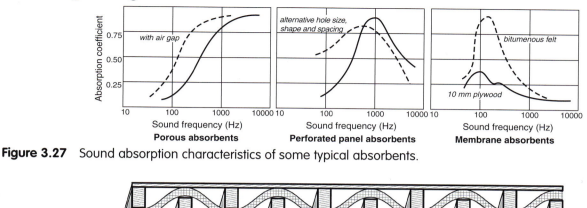

Figure 3.27 Sound absorption characteristics of some typical absorbents.

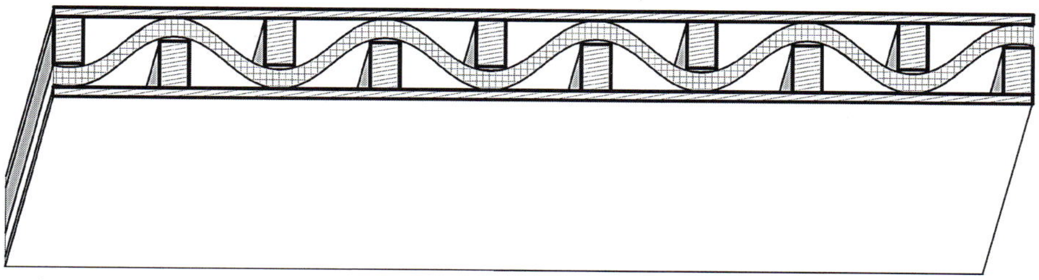

Figure 3.28 Section through a staggered stud acoustic wall.

after a certain period of use. Some of them are also highly toxic or corrosive.

No fully satisfying solution has been found yet. As with radiant cooling roof systems, desiccant systems await a cheap and reliable solution to the problem of operating the system, i.e. moving screens for temporal exposure/insulation. In the early 1980s, solar-regenerated desiccant dehumidification was a new field and complete economic analyses were not available. Today, such systems have gained acceptance although their feasibility still can be questioned.

3.4.3.5 Materials assisting in noise control

Building materials have to be looked at also from an acoustic property point of view. Sound impedance (the material's sound insulating quality) is related to the surface density and the speed of sound in the material. Generally, the greater the mass of the material, the greater the impedance ratio and the higher the sound attenuation. As a rough rule of thumb, a doubling of surface density is required to improve sound insulation by 5–6 dB in the mid-frequency range. The transmission of sound through an element varies also with the angle of incidence – being lowest at the normal incidence and greatest at the glancing or oblique one. In various materials, it also varies with different frequencies. Some building elements show better absorption of sound in a low-frequency range and better reflection of high-frequency sounds; others have opposite characteristics. Generally, low-density porous materials are good absorbers of high-frequency sounds and to absorb low- and/or medium-frequency sounds as well they must be relatively thick. Considerable improvement of the latter characteristic can be achieved with 'Helmholz' resonators, membrane or panel absorbers, or perforated panelling over porous materials. Staggered stud systems are also beneficial as is any double-leaf wall arrangement where surface impedances are utilised (Figures 3.27 and 3.28).

3.5
Functional programmes

Key recommendations in brief:

- Determine type of activities performed within a given space;
- Consider different indoor climate requirements attached to different functions;
- Adjust cooling needs in accordance with time of use and activities performed within the space;
- Offer open-air spaces for dining, entertainment and sleeping/rest.

To be effective, modification of design information based on climatic data (as suggested in Section 3.2) should be supported by adjustments based on usage type. The energy used in buildings is tied to and influenced by the building usage patterns. Different functions, such as dwelling, work, leisure, and others, create different use patterns and have different related requirements. In terms of building physics, tourist facilities are among those buildings that pose design problems of the highest complexity. One example of this is the indoor environment–function interrelationship. It is possible to identify a number of different functions that require very different approaches while dealing with the design of their respective environments. The major functional groups in the resort are:

- sleeping;
- recreational activities of various intensities;
- dining;
- food processing/cooking;
- cold storage;
- (non-cooled) storage;
- office work; and
- laundering.

Looking at the way that a tourist facility in the tropics operates, basic differences are visible in the time, duration and manner in which the spaces for housing these functions are used. Subsequently, volume and the usual occupation time of these spaces also vary. Normally, enclosed spaces in a tourist resort would include (Figure 3.29):

Spaces used mostly at night (volume of typically sized rooms is given in parentheses):

- small one-, two- or four-bed guest rooms, commonly detached or in detached groups (20–50 m^3)

Spaces used during the day and at night:

- bathrooms and toilets in guest units (5–15 m^3);

- (non-cooled) storage space (15–100 m^3);
- cold storage enclosures, usually in groups (10–50 m^3)

Spaces used mostly during the day:

- reception and lobby (200–250 m^3);
- dining room (250–400 m^3);
- kitchen (100–200 m^3);

Spaces used in the daytime only:

- office rooms (20–40 m^3);
- laundry (30–50 m^3);
- service rooms (15–20 m^3).

Spaces used mostly at night require design strategies supporting fairly quick heat dissipation. Effective cross-ventilation (coupling to a heat sink such as night air or ground) and envelope design (enabling rapid heat transfers) are among the most suitable design strategies. Spaces used mostly during the day have to be designed with heat gain prevention as the principal strategy. Adequate shading and perimeter insulation are among the most successful simple passive means of achieving this. Spaces used both during the day and at night will benefit from strategies that best respond to the mixed requirements of limiting solar heat gains and promoting heat losses whenever external temperatures drop. Furthermore, it is absolutely necessary to realise the extent of required intervention into the indoor environment. Not every space in the resort requires cooling or heating and, when it does, the requirement does not extend to all times.

The following discussion introduces proposed design adjustments to the comfort range of temperatures calculated from thermal neutralities (equation 2.1) expanded by 2.5 K. The suggested adjustments should be understood as an illustration of thermal tolerances to be expected within the given space, thus indicating scope for the apparent cooling/heating need (compare Figure 2.8).

Both the kitchen and laundry in a resort are used all day long and have numerous heat and vapour input sources. They can be conveniently located, quite often in separate building(s). However, in the resort's kitchen (and to some extent in the laundry) constraints of hygiene are also stricter and full clothing is required (approx. 0.5–0.6 Clo). Also, activities performed in both these spaces raise one's metabolic

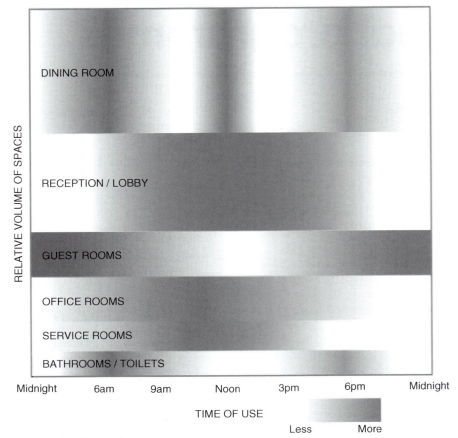

Figure 3.29 Time of use and volume of various resort rooms.

rate to not less than 2.5 Met or 145.5 W/m^2, pushing the range of acceptable temperatures down the scale by some 8 K (intensive cooling of the space is required) – in comparison to the thermally neutral temperatures calculated with the use of comfort equations (see Section 2.1). For instance, if $T_o = 30°C$, then $T_n = 28.4 °C$ and the range of acceptable temperatures in a kitchen or laundry after adjustment is 20.4°C 2.5 K. This means that these spaces should be designed for the range of approximately 18–23°C calculated after disregarding heat input from their equipment in operation.

It should be noted that kitchens and laundries are staffed by local residents who normally are not willing to compromise on their working environment conditions. This combination makes the kitchen, followed closely by the laundry, probably the most demanding place in the whole resort in terms of indoor climate control. It is not tourists, however, that we are concerned about here. The comfort sensations of local residents are more predictable and have been better researched; hence the task of designing the appropriate environment is somewhat easier. The

problem lies in the functional separation of spaces with such high heat and humidity incidence from the rest of the resort while maintaining the integrity the resort's site plan.

A resort's dining room is used by large numbers of people at meal times. Guests are usually required to put on some clothing that builds the clothing insulation up to a value of 0.4–0.5 Clo. As the metabolic rate corresponding to this activity level is around 1.2 Met or 69.8 W/m^2, in given conditions the design range can be adjusted up to +1 K in comparison to neutral temperatures. This can be read as the possibility to relax the cooling requirement for this space a little without much discomfort to the users.

It is in the bedrooms, however, where design for comfort is most important. Despite similarities with residential buildings, one can point to a number of significant differences. Bedrooms in a resort are definitely multi-functional however, they serve their principal purpose almost exclusively at night. Sleeping and resting are the activities that take place here and these can be rated at 0.7–0.8 Met or 40.7–46.5 W/m^2 metabolic rate level at night, i.e. the lower end of

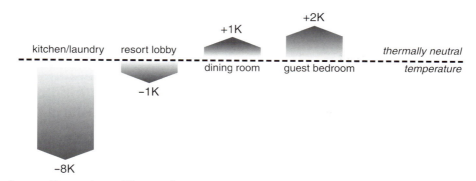

Figure 3.30 Function vs. thermal conditions adjustment.

the outdoor temperature spectrum. This value is opposed to a bedroom in a family house, which tends to be used as a study or playroom for a big part of afternoons during the week and all day at the weekends. Thus, possible adjustment of the temperature range, for which the resort bedroom should be designed, may be as high as +2 K thermal in comparison to temperatures considered thermally neutral in a given location.

This recommendation can be translated into a very relaxed requirement for cooling since much of the adjustment comes with, and is supported by, regular night-time drops in temperature. For example, if the average outdoor temperature for January (the hottest month) in Cairns, northern Australia is 28.1°C, thermal neutrality for this month is 27.7°C and the adjusted range of 'design temperatures' is around 27.2–32.2°C meaning that, probably, no cooling at all will be required. This suggestion is very much in agreement with some research carried out in the region (Bromberek, 1999).

A resort's lobby can have quite a complex functional purpose. On the one hand, it is a reception area where the arrival and departure of guests is taken care of and as such is a workplace for the administration staff of the resort. For security reasons, the place would usually be staffed 24 hours a day, 365 days a year. On the other hand, it is often a meeting place for groups and individuals involved in various activities both organised by the resort and informally. The staff and arriving and departing guests would be relatively heavily clothed (not less than 0.5 Clo), and activities performed (light office work) would be at 1.35 Met or 78.6 W/m^2 metabolic rate. These factors combined require temperatures to be adjusted to around −1 K. This kind of cooling is easily achievable by opening the lobby to allow breezes through (Figure 3.30).

Rooms in a resort vary not only in size and time of use but also in requirements concerning temperature, humidity, lighting, air exchange and other characteristics. Hence the answer to a fundamental question: 'Do the conditions provided throughout a tourist facility and/or at all times have to be uniform?' can only be 'No'. The only appropriate approach would be to tailor the provided conditions to the documented needs. This should be understood as defining these needs and determining the adequate response.

3.0–3.3 m, which allows hot air to rise above the usable volume height. Making the room higher significantly increases the cost and adds to the difficulty of stabilising the structure; it can be recommended only if cathedral ceilings are used and the increase in height is a natural consequence of this design arrangement.

The only 'modern addition' to design considerations in resorts is the issue of universal access. The access for people of various vision or mobility abilities is a concern that requires adjustment of unit design in terms of installation of access ramps, doorway widths, direction of the door opening and room to manoeuvre around it, sufficient space provided in bathrooms, location of switches and a few others. Being dependent on help from the resort staff is not a desirable option and the universal access issues are clearly a designer's responsibility (Figures 3.31–3.34).

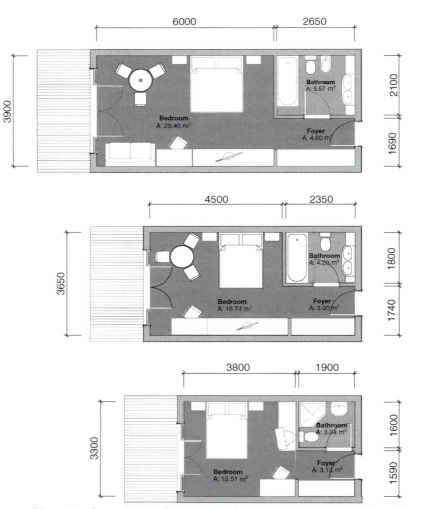

Figure 3.31 Typical sizes and layouts of resort units for 2–3 people: a. high-grade; b. mid-grade; c. budget.

Room design

A. Straight air path resulting in poor air wash

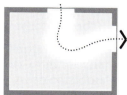

B. Openings too close – poor ventilation

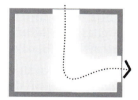

C. Much improved ventilation due to openings moved away from each other

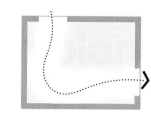

D. Wall close to openings 'attracts' flowing air

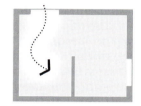

E. The worst situation – only minimal area is being ventilated

F. Openings away from each other but too close to walls create large still-air area

Figure 3.32 Air wash achieved in various configurations of openings.

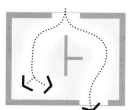

A. In 'open plan', air wash is determined by position of openings

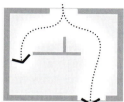

B. Partition placed in a static zone has little effect on air path

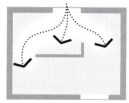

C. Partition placed in air path absorbs dynamic force of moving air

D. Partition splits flowing air, resulting in reasonable ventilation

E. Uneven distribution of air-flows caused by partition dividing incoming air

F. This partition totally blocks air path

Figure 3.33 Airflow through the plan with partitioning walls.

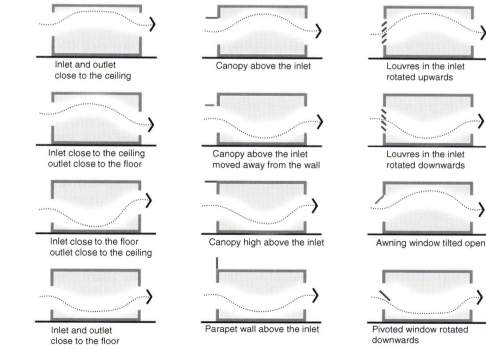

Inlet and outlet close to the ceiling

Inlet close to the ceiling outlet close to the floor

Inlet close to the floor outlet close to the ceiling

Inlet and outlet close to the floor

Canopy above the inlet

Canopy above the inlet moved away from the wall

Canopy high above the inlet

Parapet wall above the inlet

Louvres in the inlet rotated upwards

Louvres in the inlet rotated downwards

Awning window tilted open

Pivoted window rotated downwards

Figure 3.34 Airflow can be vertically redirected by a variety of controlling measures.

Transportation of holidaymakers and supplies should use carefully plotted routes and vehicles/vessels using electric rather than internal combustion engines. Where the latter seem unavoidable, they should be placed in soundproofed enclosures. Parts of the resort that are sources of increased noise levels by the nature of their function, for instance dining areas or swimming pools, should use buffers created by dense vegetation planted around them, and be moved away from areas where noise impacts are most disturbing. Other resort buildings should use natural mufflers, such as the sound of waves, whenever possible.

The problem of light pollution is often underestimated even in eco-resorts. Artificial light in the resort can be used for security reasons or for users' convenience in periods of daylight absence or simply when daylight is insufficient. Light pollution, i.e. light introduced in places and/or at times artificially superimposed on the natural cycles of daylight availability, however, can cause serious environmental damage by invading wildlife habitats and disrupting animals' normal living patterns. This is particularly evident in coastal areas where incorrect placement and excessive intensities of artificial lighting can influence the behaviour of animals kilometres away. Turtles, whales and many sea birds are particularly sensitive to non-natural light sources. To limit the impact it is highly recommended that only minimum artificial lighting be provided and that this should light minimum areas at the lowest usable illuminance.

Outdoor lighting should be avoided and even interior luminaires should be placed so that their visibility through openings is limited. Motion sensor activated lamps should be used instead of continuous all-night lighting of areas sensitive from a safety or security point of view. Driveways should have reflective posts installed along the edges rather than lit ones. Great care should be taken to ensure that light beams are task directed and that upward ones are cut off entirely. All lighting that potentially could be visible from the sea should be excluded. Windows facing the beach should have heavy tinting or opaque blinds installed for light control. In places where lighting is unavoidable vegetation should be planted with the aim of limiting its obtrusiveness.

Part Four
Case Studies

A study of several different resorts in various tropical locations was conducted to investigate a selection of designs, randomised from the environmental response by design point of view. This review also delivered information about the current understanding of eco-tourism principles in the surveyed regions as well as revealing current trends and attitudes among tropical resort stakeholders: designers, developers and operators. The study uncovered a large variety of buildings being used for accommodating eco-tourists. In virtually all eco-resorts, designers decided to dip into the richness of the vernacular architecture treasure trove for inspiration and to visibly mark them as environmentally-friendly developments.

It appears, however, that using the vocabulary of the vernacular does not necessarily mean that developers fully understand the role of all the features or the benefits of using this approach in their modern adaptations. For example, certain features that will have an obvious and significant impact on the indoor environment, such as roof monitors, thick insulation in the roof, effective cross-ventilation or high ceilings, were often introduced in the investigated resorts quite by accident, rather than by intention. Sometimes they were an artefact of copying fashionably traditional forms and sometimes they came about only through the developer using local labour because they were unaware of building in any other way. Some of these highly effective elements have been subsequently removed from the comfort equation by sealing the indoor environment in order to have effective air-conditioning, if demanded.

The end result is a haphazard mixture of passive design features either performing their original role by happenstance or being reduced to mere ornaments. Despite this, the study results indicate that many of these incidental creations do in fact cope reasonably well with the tropical climate, at least during the night-time. Many apparent errors in this approach to design do not necessarily render the resultant indoor conditions unacceptable either, at least not over brief periods of time. But, even allowing for the relative success of the somewhat indiscriminate and unsystematic application of various regimes and technologies, one is left with the distinct feeling that it should be possible to do the job better with a more informed approach.

The study did not find justification for air-conditioning, particularly in those tropical resorts laying claim to 'environmental friendliness'. To begin with, indoor conditions, which are much the same as the average tropical weather outside, seldom are uncomfortable enough to require a mechanical device to modify them. Running air-conditioning in a typical resort location is expensive, both in the financial and in the environmental sense of the word. Fuel-powered systems generate noise and pollution, and fuel supply (to remote locations in particular) carries an inherent danger of fuel spills and other environmental hazards. Moreover, numerous examples from vernacular architecture have delivered sufficient proof that comfort in the tropics is achievable with passive measures only. It should also be stressed that eco-tourists are usually happy to adjust their behaviour and thus reduce any perceived discomfort; ultimately, they can leave the resort at short notice. It is a low price to pay for being truly environmentally-friendly.

There is a widespread belief among experts that passive climate control solutions are economically and environmentally justifiable alternatives to mechanical systems, and this applies in the tropics as well. It seems that traditional biases against tropical conditions may have been built upon experiences derived from instances where resorts have simply been built to a wrong or inappropriate design. The review reported in the following pages delivers further proof that indoor conditions in the tropics can fall well within the comfort range without mechanical support.

It is worth noting that each of the case study resorts has features that make them worth listing in this review. They are among the best examples of eco-resorts in their respective regions. If not actually strictly, they provide a well-meaning interpretation of environmental friendliness in their design and application.

4.0
A question of practicality

The following case studies are a cross-section of various attempts at somewhat more eco-friendly approaches to design and operation of resorts in the tropics. The author visited 15 tropical resorts in four countries in November and December 2005. The period was a transitional 'between the seasons' time, when temperatures are usually close to annual averages. In fact, in all but one location annual minima were lower than the observed minimum temperatures and annual maxima were higher only in the Mexican locations. The timing of the visits corresponded with 'early summer' in the southern hemisphere and 'early winter' in the northern. Precipitation is the main indicator of the seasonal change in the tropics, even if the frequency and intensity of the rainfall is more often determined by the specifics of the location, for instance its topography. Precipitation directly influences relative humidity (RH) but readings of RH taken during the study tour were consistently very high, even if significant rainfall during the visit was noted only in some Fiji and Cook Islands locations.

The resorts were selected because of claims of their 'environmental friendliness'. Their locations also represented a fairly typical selection of tourist destinations in the tropics, with all but one resort built directly on a beach. The environmental friendliness claims were investigated, various design features were photographed and/or described, operational data were collected, managing staff were interviewed and air temperature readings were taken both inside and outside the allocated unit over 24-hour periods, together with relative humidity readings indoors. Four of the visited resorts were found to be no different from other resorts in the area, and therefore to have no basis for the claimed eco-friendly status. Subsequently, they were discarded from the sample. Eight of the remaining eleven are presented in more detail in the following pages.

A digital thermometer/hygrometer with memory was used in the assessment of thermal conditions found during the visits. The use of device memory allowed the recording of the highest and the lowest temperatures as well as the highest and the lowest relative humidity readings during the diurnal cycle of the visit. The indoor temperature and RH readings were taken at the bedside at bed mattress height (approximately 0.5 m above the floor). If there was air-conditioning and/or a fan in the unit, they remained switched off during the entire period. All windows fitted with fly-screens, on the other hand, remained open during the night (see Section 2.1.2 for the negative effect on airflow produced by fly-screens). External temperatures were measured directly outside the allocated unit. Since the Stevenson screen was not available, attempts were made to find a spot shaded during the entire day for this purpose. The temperature readings are presented in Table 4.1 (RH readings were over 95 per cent, at least at some point in time during the night, in all locations).

Half of the resorts visited offered mechanical air-conditioning (AC) in guest accommodation as an option. Despite their environmental claims, managers in nearly all resorts were willing to provide air-conditioners as they felt 'compelled by their markets' to do so. Furthermore, in all resorts that offered AC, room service was instructed to ensure that the air-conditioner was switched on before a new guest arrived (generating a rather negative impression of eco-friendliness and a big impact on energy demand: see Section 2.1). All the managers admitted in their interviews that the cost of providing AC was very high. Nevertheless, AC has not been seen as a factor having an impact on the environment.

The 'eco-resort' status was seen as being achievable through strategies such as controlling tourist impacts, using natural building materials or blending their resorts, as a business endeavour, with the local community. Impacts from a resort's operations, including noise and pollution generated by a power plant, were seldom perceived as being part of the 'eco-friendly' package. Even less so were the environmental costs of providing supplies, for instance fuel. It is worth noting that due to the unreliable nature of their power generation capabilities, fuel-free power generators would usually be supported by back-up diesel generators – even in eco-friendly resorts.

Not a single resort amongst those visited was designed to utilise passive means of climate control. Features coming from vernacular architecture that were replicated in their designs often seemed superficial and dishonest (the pastiche approach). An example was a palm leaf thatch covering metal decking on a roof to give it a traditional hut appearance, or a roof monitor blocked to seal the interior for effective air-conditioning. Yet in nearly all instances

Table 4.1 Comparison of climatic annual averages with temperatures indoors and outdoors, corresponding Humidex indices and comfort ranges in the studied locations

Resort location	Air-cond. availability	Minimum temperature (°C)				Maximum temperature (°C)				Humidex index[b]	Thermal neutrality[c]
		Average[a]	In	Out	Diff.	Average[a]	In	Out	Diff.		
Vanua Levu, Fiji	Yes	21.6[1]	26.4	26.1	+0.3	27.9[1]	29.1	31.1	−2.0	34.3	26.4
Naigani, Fiji	No	22.4[2]	25.9	23.5	+2.4	29.0[2]	34.9	33.0	+1.9	37.3	26.9
Rarotonga 1, Cook Islands	No	21.9[3]	25.9	25.6	+0.3	26.3[3]	30.0	30.9	−0.9	34.5	26.2
Rarotonga 2, Cook Islands	Yes	21.9[3]	25.9	23.9	+2.0	26.3[3]	29.4	29.6	−0.2	34.2	26.2
Aitutaki, Cook Islands	No	22.1[4]	27.4	26.9	+0.5	28.8[4]	34.5	32.6	+1.9	37.9	26.8
Moorea, French Polynesia	Yes	21.0[5]	27.4	26.1	+1.3	30.7[5]	32.0	32.3	−0.3	36.5	26.9
Bora Bora, French Polynesia	Yes	23.4[6]	28.9	27.4	+1.5	29.0[6]	30.9	33.6	−2.7	36.7	27.0
Tulúm, Mexico	No	20.9[7]	21.3	18.9	+2.4	30.9[7]	27.6	28.0	−0.4	30.5	26.0
Bahía Permejo, Mexico	No	21.9[8]	24.6	22.9	+1.7	30.5[8]	27.4	26.4	+1.0	32.3	25.9
Rio Indio, Mexico	No	21.9[8]	24.6	24.3	+0.3	30.5[8]	27.4	26.6	+0.8	32.3	25.9
Chichén Itzá, Mexico	Yes	19.3[9]	26.0	23.9	+2.1	32.5[9]	30.1	29.9	+0.2	34.6	25.6
Average for 11 resorts		21.7	25.8	24.5	+1.3	29.3	30.3	30.4	−0.1	34.6	26.4

[a] Annual average minimum/maximum temperature at a meteorological station nearest to the resort: 1-Savusavu, 2-Nausori, 3-Avarua, 4-Ootu, 5-Papeete, 6-Motu Mute, 7-Tulúm, 8-Chetumal, 9-Dzitas.

[b] Humidex index as calculated for the observed indoor air temperatures.

[c] Determined with the Nicol's equation (see Section 2.1, eqn (2.1)); results in this column ±2 deg give 80 percentile acceptability; compare this with the observed night-time (minimum) air temperatures indoors.

the indoor climate was remarkably comfortable. Minimum (i.e. night-time) indoor temperatures recorded were always higher than the corresponding temperatures outdoors. This effect of building mass was most evident in the heavyweight structures of the Rarotonga 2, Tulúm, Bahía Permejo and Chichén Itzá resorts. Even these higher indoor temperatures were within the comfort range determined by the thermal neutrality equation (see Chapter 2.1). In the only resort where the night-time temperature was outside the range, it was actually lower than the ones called for by the equation (Table 4.1).

The author's own perceptions were in line with predictions arrived at using the Humidex index. Mild discomfort was felt in conditions resulting in Humidex values of 36.5 or more (as in three out of the eleven resorts surveyed). However, the perceptions were based on conditions achieved with no air-conditioning or fan working in the unit. Cross-ventilation was not always possible, either. It is easy to imagine that the conditions would be greatly improved if only a slight air movement was induced or, better still, if the resorts were designed to depend chiefly on passive climate control.

Most resorts relied on cross-ventilation, cathedral ceilings and, in a few instances, shading to create comfortable indoor conditions. This did not seem a deliberate part of some 'grand plan' to utilise passive design features. Instead, it seemed more like the accidental result of pursuing a romantic image that some of these resorts wished to evoke by reference to the vernacular. As one of the resort owners put it, 'Tourists come to my resort for a dream and I'm selling them that dream'. Lack of understanding of visitors' comfort perceptions in tropical climates was also evident. When one of the managers agreed to a little experiment involving raising the temperature in his air-conditioned office by three degrees (to a level suggested by Nicol's equation discussed in Section 2.1), he was genuinely surprised how cool it felt after only a brief walk outside. His experience, on which he was basing his decisions about temperature settings for AC in guest units, was derived from working in the office all day long.

Findings from earlier research by the author suggest that passive climate control should involve specific requirements of the users. It should also exploit the identified differences between tourists, who are only short-term visitors to the tropics, and the residents of the region. The study strengthened the opinion that relative comfort is achievable in the tropics without help from mechanical devices. In all the resorts studied, night-time conditions, when extracted from all-day averages, fell within the comfort range determined by Nicol's equation.

In all resorts, some degree of discomfort was predicted with the Humidex index (for more detail on Humidex see Section 2.1); the average score of 34.6 indicates that the discomfort would only be mild for most tourists and, allowing for their attitudes, could be acceptable to them during a short-term visit. There

at the single building level	Resort:	1	2	3	4	5	6	7	8
Features supporting cross-ventilation: open plan and ample apertures		✔	✔	✔	✔	✔	✔	✔	
Room height and/or features supporting stack effect ventilation		✔	✔	✔	✔	✔	✔	✔	
Informed use of slats and louvres		✔	✔		✔				
Features providing sufficient daylight levels		✔	✔	✔	✔	✔		✔	
Careful orientation to avoid overheating							✔		
Extensive use of shading by vegetation and/or terrain features		✔	✔					✔	✔	✔
Building raised off the ground			✔	✔	✔				
Open-air covered space available for rest and/or other purposes			✔	✔				✔	✔
Deliberate use of colour and texture influencing perception of indoor climate		✔	✔	✔	✔	✔	✔		✔
Energy-efficient lighting		✔	✔	✔	✔	✔	✔	✔	✔
Solar water heating		✔						✔	
Extensive use of locally sourced natural materials		✔	✔	✔	✔	✔	✔	✔	✔
Extensive use of materials requiring little or no maintenance		✔	✔	✔	✔	✔	✔	✔	✔
Extensive use of recycled materials								✔	✔

Figure 4.1 Summary of environment-friendly features in the case study resorts; building level and resort level.

Figure 4.1.1 General view of the resort from its pier. Traditional thatched roofs blend well with the tropical island surroundings.

The integrated biosystems and functional landscapes were designed to support energy sustainability, integrated food production, water conservation and waste reduction strategies. At the same time, the resort's operators are very sensitive to the fact that they are guests and members of the local community, and thus obliged to accept certain social responsibilities. In a very real sense, the operators and the local people have been partners in the resort's development and subsequent operations. The dialogue is ongoing to ensure compatibility of the facility with the regional culture, local traditions and community's aspirations for the future (Figure 4.1.2).

4.1.2 Site selection and landscaping

The underpinning philosophy was to keep additional development to a minimum and to make better use of what already exists. The JMC resort has taken advantage of an existing facility and revitalised it to meet new standards. The retrofitting process took the form of recycling, reuse and upgrading of a prime site resort constructed on the theme of a traditional Fijian village. The local natural habitats have also been restored in the process. The village theme was considered critical to the design ethic as it dignified the cultural heritage and utilised design features refined by generations to meet unique Fijian geography

and climate. The total site area is around 17 acres (almost 7 ha) (Figure 4.1.3).

Landscape management is seen as particularly important because of the potential for various coastal impacts. The original mangrove habitats are being restored to prevent erosion. Permanent ponds have been created to replace seasonal puddles of standing water. This helps to control mosquitoes as well as provides diverse animal and plant ecosystems. Recent tests showed a 100-fold reduction of mosquito larvae in the pond compared with the puddles. Edible landscaping is being implemented and it is estimated that once fully functional it will save the resort $1000 per month by growing fruit, vegetables and herbs on site. Passion fruit vines are used to provide visual privacy between *bures*. Thoughtful area lighting is used sparingly to limit light pollution.

4.1.3 Construction and materials

Principal materials used in the development include local timbers, palm-leaf thatch, ceramic tiles, stone and concrete. The choice was guided by a number of principles: to minimise impact on the landscape, to use natural materials and systems when possible, to use materials fabricated in an environmentally responsible manner, to minimise construction waste and, finally, to design for flexibility and implement

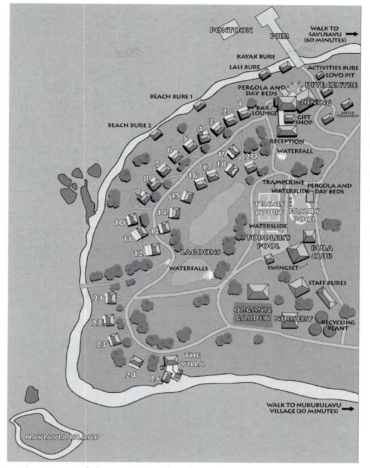

Figure 4.1.2   Plan of the resort (courtesy of the JMC Fiji Islands Resort).

more environmental technologies and systems as they become available. The materials and technologies used also employ local building knowledge and skills thus minimising the need for external expertise, providing local artisans with employment as well as cultivating and preserving local traditions (Figures 4.1.4–5).

4.1.4 Energy management

Passive solar design maximises the utilisation of nature's free services to cool and refresh the air, to heat water and dry the laundry. Thatched roofs, high ceilings, louvred windows and shading vegetation deliver the entire required air-conditioning (air-conditioners are not provided in guest rooms). Solar hot water systems and solar assisted systems deliver hot water during most of the year. The remaining required energy comes from the town grid powered by a hydroelectric power station. A wind monitoring station, established in cooperation with the Fijian Department of Energy, looks to wind as an additional source of power, perhaps supplemented by photovoltaic cell banks, in the future. Energy-efficient compact fluorescent and halogen lighting is used throughout the resort together with energy-efficient appliances. A solar oven is used for native food cooking demonstrations and in children's programmes.

4.1.5 Water management

Water management includes a number of strategies for water conservation and water pollution prevention. Used water is treated in constructed wetlands and reused in irrigation systems. The objective is to

Figure 4.1.3   *Bures* (guest units) strung along the shoreline enjoy good sea breezes and visual privacy.

Figures 4.1.4–5   Thatched roof over the dining area; constructed, maintained and repaired by the local craftspeople.

Figure 4.1.6   Dining halls at the JMC resort are open-air traditional Fijian structures. The pool deck also doubles as a dining space at dinner time.

keep nutrients cycling in the system rather than releasing them into the sea. Further purified, treated fertilised water is used in fruit and vegetable gardens and ultimately returns as wastewater, completing the cycle. Both the constructed wetlands and multi-crop agricultural systems are based on strategies developed and coordinated with the international University of South Pacific to ensure that the tried theory and developed practices will be of use to others in the region (Figure 4.1.6).

4.1.6 Waste management

Waste minimisation, reuse and recycling are at the core of the resort's operations. Grey water, kitchen waste and sewage are considered resources to be utilised for beneficial purposes. Staff education and buying procedures dramatically reduce packaging waste. Local staff find uses for most cardboard and metal packaging, and waste is limited primarily to plastics. A local distributor of bottled water recycles plastic bottles and recyclers in the Fijian capital of Suva recycle paper and batteries. Furthermore, photographic processing chemicals are rendered inert and the silver

is extracted and sent to Suva for reuse. Nearly all kitchen waste is composted.

The major difficulty with adequate waste management, as identified by the resort, is that due to the resort's efficiency its waste stream became so small as to be rendered uneconomical to process by specialised companies. Consequently, the resort is cooperating with local schools and businesses in the nearby town of Savusavu to increase, for instance, paper volume to a level sufficient for an external enterprise to become interested in getting involved (Figures 4.1.7–8).

4.1.7 The control of other impacts

New construction was kept to a minimum and an attempt was made not to impair the visual environment, in particular the scenic views out to the bay.

The resort uses carefully selected non-toxic chemicals on a limited scale. Chemical fertilisers are not used. The use of pesticides and insecticides has been reduced by 90 per cent in comparison to similar areas in the region. Guests are educated about the environmental impact of totally eliminating tropical wildlife

Figures 4.1.7–8   The design of individual guest units is based on traditional Fijian houses. Their high cathedral ceilings, lightweight thatched roofs and generous louvred windows on both long sides ensure an excellent thermal environment even without air-conditioning.

encroaching on their space (ants, cockroaches and geckos), to understand the unavoidable consequences of such actions. The pest management programme uses pest parasitoids and breeding habitat reduction as a means of control.

All dive sites are rotated, with some of them temporarily closed, to control diver impacts. When in use, they all have moorings to prevent damage from boat anchors. Others are only accessible to experienced eco-divers.

The resort conducts regular seminars for staff as an essential part of its environmental ethic. The popular perception of luxury associated with carelessness and waste is challenged to make up for the bad examples the world conveyed to them about so-called 'success'. The resort owners are also committed to disseminating ideas and findings throughout the wider region. A relationship established with the University of South

Pacific allows educational benefits to spread beyond the island of Vanua Levu or even Fiji.

4.1.8 The resort's climatic performance

During the visit to the resort in late November (early summer), the external temperatures ranged from 26.1–31.1°C and corresponding internal temperatures (with fans switched off) were in the range 26.4–29.1°C. This indicates minimal heat storage and short time lag occurring in some materials used in *bures* (ceramic tiles on concrete floor slab) as well as fairly efficient shading and natural ventilation – dampening temperatures indoors by a sensible two-degree margin.

at the single unit level

Visual pollution				
Light pollution				
Noise pollution				
Airborne pollution				
Thermal environment-related impacts				
Impacts on geology of the site				
Impacts on soil: compacting, contamination				
Impacts on water: surface, underground sources, run-off				
Impacts on the original vegetation				
Impacts on the wildlife				

at the resort level

Visual pollution				
Light pollution				
Noise pollution				
Airborne pollution				
Thermal environment-related impacts				
Impacts on geology of the site				
Impacts on soil: compacting, contamination				
Impacts on water: surface, underground sources, run-off				
Impacts on the original vegetation				
Impacts on the wildlife				
Socio-economic dependencies				

Figure 4.1.9   The extent of the resort's potential environmental impacts. (**Note:** The extent of the resort's impacts [ranging from positive through neutral to negative] should be read in conjunction with the information in Figure 4.1).

4.1.9 Concluding remarks

The most important feature of the Jean-Michel Cousteau Fiji Islands Resort is its integration with the local community. The resort is designed to support and be supported by the local community. It draws on local building knowledge, local traditions and local building materials. Design of guest units (*bures*) follows the design of traditional huts utilising some of their advantageous characteristics, such as very high cathedral ceilings and thatched roofs. *Bures* are strung along the shoreline taking in breezes coming from the sea. Native vegetation provides hedges, which act as both a visual and acoustic barrier between the units. Also, planning issues are well resolved, with dining rooms (doubling as an entertainment area) and playgrounds for the children moved well away from the 'residential' part. Finally, most of resort operations are in tune with the overall image of this multi-award winning resort. The ostentatious opulence could draw some criticism and guests could also be more prominently encouraged to open their units up to the environment, but the overall assessment of the JMC as an eco-resort could not be more positive (Figure 4.1.9).

4.2
Are Tamanu Beach Hotel and Muri Beach Hideaway

Are Tamanu Beach Hotel

Location:	Amuri Village, Aitutaki, Cook Islands
Year of completion:	2001
Total cost of construction:	US$1.2 million (approx.)
Architect/designer:	Des Eggelton of Frame Group, Cook Islands
Consultant:	Michael Henry
Builder:	Maru Ben
Number of guest units:	12 self-contained *ares* (studio bungalows)
Maximum number of guests:	30 (approx.)
Other facilities on site:	café-bar, office, laundry
Site area:	1 acre (0.4 ha)
Access methods:	by road (from Rarotonga International airport or Aitutaki atoll harbour)
Principal attractions in the area:	the lagoon and reefs of Aitutaki atoll, the island's nature, water sports

Muri Beach Hideaway

Location:	Muri Beach, Rarotonga, Cook Islands
Year of completion:	2001
Total cost of construction:	US$400 K(approx.)
Architect/designer:	Des Eggelton of Frame Group, Cook Islands (concept by Mike Henry) in cooperation with Pauline MacFarlane (resort owner and manager)
Builder:	local craftspeople
Number of guest units:	5 self-contained studio bungalows
Max. number of guests:	10
Other facilities on site:	office, laundry, owner/manager accommodation
Site area:	0.375 acres (0.15 ha)
Access methods:	by road (from Rarotonga International airport at Avarua)
Principal attractions in the area:	the lagoon and reefs, culture and art tours, dining

4.2.1 In their own words

Are Tamanu Beach Village has a history going back hundreds of years. Like all lands in the Cook Islands, the land the [resort] is built on has a traditional name and it is Are Tamanu. The literal translation of Are Tamanu is 'House of the Mahogany Tree' and this land still retains some of the native mahogany trees from which it is named (Figure 4.2.1).

In keeping with its name, Are Tamanu's luxurious self-catering individual *ares* feature tamanu floors and Cook Island style thatched roofs. Tamanu is also used for the carvings in each room and is a feature of the popular poolside bar.

[The resort's] private white sand beach borders Aitutaki's superb lagoon providing endless opportunities for swimming, snorkelling and canoeing. Around [the] freshwater swimming pool is a large deck providing a pleasurable venue for evening cocktails and Sunday BBQs.

[All] individual *ares* offer first class appointments including luxurious king-size beds, full kitchens, refrigerator/freezer, gas cooker, microwave oven, quality cutlery and crockery, and IDD telephones.

Each *are* has a separate bathroom with hairdryer, kitchen, breakfast bar, room safe and outdoor decks with dining settings for four. All rooms are air-conditioned and have insect screened windows. [Source: Are Tamanu Beach Hotel] (Figure 4.2.2).

The Muri Beach Hideaway is an example of a small owner-operated resort. Apart from the original building – a two-storey family house, doubling nowadays as a laundry, storage space and the owner's accommodation – there are only five small bungalows built on the site. The Are Tamanu, on the other hand, is a fairly typical medium-size resort, more than twice the size of its Rarotongan counterpart. Both share the same unit design with only a few small modifications introduced at the Muri Beach Hideaway.

4.2.2 Site selection and landscaping

Both resorts are sited in locations of a suburban character, and resort development has brought about an improvement rather than destruction of the original sites. Both sites were already extensively modified before the resorts were built.

The Are Tamanu is located on the principal island of Aitutaki atoll, on the major road running

Figure 4.2.1 Both the Are Tamanu and the Muri Beach Hideaway share the same bungalow design; the resorts differ in size, positioning, some material and operational details as well as in landscaping design.

Figure 4.2.2 The Muri Beach Hideaway started as an ordinary suburban block. The original house is still in use as the owner/manager's accommodation, storage space and a service block.

north–south along the west coast linking the airport with the major settlements of Amuri, Ureia, Arutanga and Reureu. In total, the site modifications amounted to 13 coconut trees being removed, several ornamental trees and bushes being planted, three large volcanic rocks being brought to the site, an in-ground swimming pool and a fish pond being built, and a few walkways being paved.

The site of the Muri Beach Hideaway is also rather typical for the area: a suburban building block wedged between the coastline and the main road on the island of Rarotonga. In fact, only a third of the block has been set aside for development; the reminder constitutes a buffer zone, nearly 150 m wide, which shields the resort from traffic on a relatively busy road. The site has been extensively modified for a number of years now. Site development included establishing tropical garden patches, planting hedges, building an in-ground freshwater swimming pool and timber decks on the waterfront as well as laying out crushed coral and sand, timber and concrete walkways.

4.2.3 Construction and materials

The bungalows are an example of a very smart and efficient use of design, which makes excellent use of natural building materials such as engineered timber products (exterior graded Fijian plywood,

Figures 4.2.3–4 The Are Tamanu resort's *are* or bungalow design is the original, on which the Muri Beach Hideaway's bungalows were based; sharing the same envelope, a few modifications appear in the Muri Beach Hideaway floor layout and material solutions.

New Zealand pine poles, bearers and joists, timber decking and flooring), palm-leaf thatch and rattan matting as well as ceramic floor tiles. Roofs at Are Tamanu are metal decking covered with thatch, in which respect they differ from the Muri Beach Hideaway. The thatch gives the units a traditional appearance and reduces the noise from the rain. Materials require minimal maintenance. The bungalow layout is also exemplary as an efficient and functional space design.

Figures 4.2.10–12 Are Tamanu's landscape design is quite typical yet efficient in the use of the narrow block of land; a central communication spine services two rows of bungalows with a beach café-bar, pool and deck at its ocean end.

Figures 4.2.13–14 The Muri Beach Hideaway replicates the basic layout of the communication scheme: a walkway services a single file of guest units due to the narrowness of the site.

4.2.5 Water management

Most of Are Tamanu's needs are covered by water coming from an artesian source through a town mains. There are also two rainwater tanks capable of storing 108 000 litres each. Water for irrigation is recycled grey water. The content of grey water from the sewage treated on site is too high in nutrients and this issue is going to be addressed in the near future by an improved purification system.

Similarly to the Aitutaki resort, the Muri Beach Hideaway water comes from town reticulation. There is also an underground rainwater tank capable of storing 10 000 litres. On average, an occupied unit uses 120 litres of water per day. Savings are achieved by restricting usage of water from the town grid to human consumption. Water for irrigation is recycled grey water. All toilets have dual flush systems and virtually all liquid waste is processed on site and recycled, depending on its source, in either flowerbeds or for fruit and vegetable patches (Figure 4.2.7).

Figures 4.2.15–16   Site edges in the two resorts represent very different approaches serving the same purpose of securing acoustic privacy and safety for the guests: Are Tamanu has a stone wall while the Muri Beach Hideaway hides behind a dense vegetation along a stream.

4.2.6 Waste management

Waste management at both resorts is similar. A local contractor takes solid waste generated at Are Tamanu away to a local tip. Liquid waste is processed underground on site. At the Muri Beach waste is collected and carted away by a local contractor to the capital town of Avarua where plastic, glass and metal waste is recycled; organic waste is composted on site. The liquid waste is processed on site in the resort's own underground sewage purifying system (Figures 4.2.8–9).

4.2.7 The resort's climatic performance

During the visit to the Muri Beach resort, very late in November (early summer), the external temperatures ranged from 25.6–30.9°C and corresponding internal temperatures (with fans switched off) were in the range 25.9–30.0°C. This indicates very efficient thermal design and nearly no heat storage in the light-weight structure of the unit. Conditions inside were very similar to those outside in the shade, i.e. without the effects of direct solar irradiation.

4.2.8 Concluding remarks

In both the Are Tamanu Beach Hotel and the Muri Beach Hideaway we can see a very clever design. Resort planning provides reasonably good – for the given conditions – views and ventilation without compromising visual or acoustic privacy. Application of building materials is smart and efficient, and energy and water are used in the best possible way. The guest units are easy to maintain and their functional layout is highly efficient.

Both resorts occupy very narrow sites. Furthermore, both are enclosed within boundaries defined by high and dense hedges. Despite being open on

at the single unit level

Visual pollution				
Light pollution				
Noise pollution				
Airborne pollution				
Thermal environment-related impacts				
Impacts on geology of the site				
Impacts on soil: compacting, contamination				
Impacts on water: surface, underground sources, run-off				
Impacts on the original vegetation				
Impacts on the wildlife				

at the resort level

Visual pollution				
Light pollution				
Noise pollution				
Airborne pollution				
Thermal environment-related impacts				
Impacts on geology of the site				
Impacts on soil: compacting, contamination				
Impacts on water: surface, underground sources, run-off				
Impacts on the original vegetation				
Impacts on the wildlife				
Socio-economic dependencies				

Figure 4.2.17   The extent of the resorts' potential environmental impacts (Note: The extent of the resort's impacts [ranging from positive through neutral to negative] should be read in conjunction with the information in Figure 4.1).

their short ocean sides, this narrowness combined with constricting vegetation severely hampers penetration of breezes and air movement through the sites (Figures 4.10–12).

The *ares* of the Are Tamanu Beach Hotel are capable of operating with or without air-conditioning – both options demanded by the targeted markets and both offered in all units. The guest units rely on air-conditioning for most of the time, however, and natural ventilation is not critical to their performance. On the other hand, the Muri Beach Hideaway units, which do not offer air-conditioning, demonstrate excellent quality of their design by providing indoor conditions well within the comfort range. They also prove that the design, shared by both, is capable of coping with the tropical climate without powered air-conditioning support (Figures 4.2.13–14, Figures 4.2.15–16, Figure 4.2.17).

4.3

Sheraton Moorea Lagoon Resort & Spa

Location:	Papetoai, Moorea, French Polynesia
Year of completion:	2001
Total cost of construction:	US$10.2 million (approx.)
Architect:	Pierre Lacombe
Consultant:	
Builder:	local craftspeople
Number of guest units:	106 bungalows (57 over-water, 42 garden, 7 beach)
Max. number of guests:	280
Other facilities on site:	offices and reception, restaurant and kitchen, spa, pool and poolside bar, 150 m² meeting room, over-water bar, beach grill and bar, fitness gym, scuba centre, two tennis courts, 12 staff accommodation, five store rooms, maintenance shed, extensive network of walkways, helipad
Site area:	7.5 acres (3 ha)
Access methods:	by road and ferry or plane from Tahiti (Papeete International airport), or helicopter from Papeete
Principal attractions in the area:	the sea, lagoon and reefs, Moorea island with its rainforest and Polynesian villages, Tahiti

4.3.1 In their own words

Sheraton Moorea Lagoon Resort & Spa is a full service resort ideally located between Morea's historical Cook's Bay and Opunohu Bay. The property offers a pristine white sand beach, crystal blue lagoon and lush tropical gardens (Figure 4.3.1).

At only 15 minutes from the airport, or 25 minutes from the ferry dock, wind your way along the scenic coast towards Papetoai. The garden and over-water bungalows are spacious, luxurious and are designed to provide maximum privacy. Double connecting bungalows are also available for larger parties travelling together or for families.

[…] The Sheraton Moorea Lagoon Resort & Spa has individual garden or twin bungalows. They are finely decorated in a Polynesian style and with exotic wood. They are located in the middle of luxuriant tropical gardens, and right next to the azure lagoon of the island of Moorea.

The bungalows are fully-equipped with modern comforts: individually-controlled air-conditioning, fan [and many other electrical appliances], private terrace. The bathroom includes a bathtub and separate shower, a hairdryer, a make-up mirror as well as American and European plugs.

- 22 garden connected bungalows (37.25 m²)
- 20 superior bungalows (35.25 m²)
- 7 beach bungalows (35.25 m²)

In the intimacy of your over-water, you will listen to the murmur of the waves and contemplate through a glass opening in the floor the perpetual ballet of multicoloured fish. If you wish to see them closer, just descend the pontoon ladder into the warm waters of the lagoon.

For even greater intimacy, you can choose to stay in our Horizon bungalows with a 180° horizon view which are located closest to the coral reef.

The bungalows are equipped with individually-controlled air-conditioning, fan, private terrace with outside shower [and a range of appliances, similar to the Garden bungalows] (Figure 4.3.2).

- 57 over-water bungalows among which 30 are Horizon bungalows (35.75 m²) [Source: Starwood Hotels].

4.3.2 Site selection and landscaping

The resort occupies a former hotel site and the area has been extensively recultivated and replanted in adaptation to its current use. Other major changes include establishing a swimming pool and a fish pond (Figure 4.3.3, Figure 4.3.4).

4.3.3 Construction

Principal building materials used at Sheraton Moorea are timber, concrete (used for piling), *maiao* (pandanus) leaves replaced on a 5-year cycle, flagstone, and

Figure 4.3.1   Like many other Polynesian resorts, Sheraton Moorea Resort & Spa offers accommodation in over-water individual bungalows.

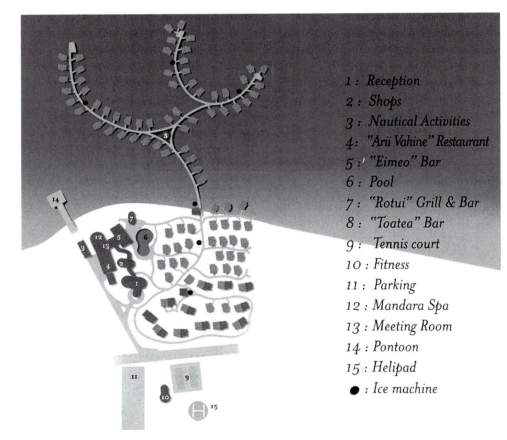

1 : *Reception*
2 : *Shops*
3 : *Nautical Activities*
4: *"Arii Vahine" Restaurant*
5 : *"Eimeo" Bar*
6 : *Pool*
7 : *"Rotui" Grill & Bar*
8 : *"Toatea" Bar*
9 : *Tennis court*
10 : *Fitness*
11 : *Parking*
12 : *Mandara Spa*
13 : *Meeting Room*
14 : *Pontoon*
15 : *Helipad*
● : *Ice machine*

Figure 4.3.2   Plan of the resort (courtesy of Sheraton Moorea Lagoon Resort & Spa).

Figure 4.3.3   Open water ponds and pools cool the reception area and adjacent restaurant.

Figure 4.3.4   The architecture of all bungalows at the resort relates to local traditions not only in form and colour but also choice of materials, with prominent pandanus thatch and extensive use of timber.

Figure 4.3.5   Detail of bamboo wall cladding.

ceramic tiles, both on floors and walls (Figure 4.3.5, Figure 4.3.6, Figure 4.3.7).

4.3.4 Operational energy

The source of power is a town grid powered from a diesel generator. The resort uses 525 kWh per month, on average, at a substantial annual cost of 1.2 million Polynesian francs (approx. US$12 500). The principal reason for such a huge demand is the large number of electrical appliances in both guest units and the rest of the resort. Energy saving is encouraged and low energy lighting is in use but future changes (extension of the banquet room, the addition of a kitchen to the beach bar and a jacuzzi to the pool area) planned by the resort will, most certainly, increase this demand even further (Figures 4.3.8–9).

4.3.5 Water management

The resort uses water from the town mains, supplementing it with rainwater from its own storage when available. The monthly cost of water supplied to the resort is 350 000 francs (approx. US$3600). This cost has started growing recently at a considerable rate and the resort's management encourages saving of this resource. All toilets are dual flush and grey water from washing is recycled in an irrigation system.

4.3.6 Waste management

Most solid waste is disposed of at the communal tip on the island. Most plastic, glass and metal waste is sorted out and recycled through a 'green programme' instigated by the local government, and organic waste is composted. The liquid waste is stored in septic tanks and removed monthly.

4.3.7 The resort's climatic performance

During the visit to the resort in early December (early summer), external temperatures ranged from 26.1–32.3°C and corresponding internal temperatures in a beachside bungalow (with air-conditioner and fans switched off) were in the range 27.4–32.0°C. This

Figure 4.3.6 Detail of roof thatch seen from the interior.

Figure 4.3.7 All bars and restaurants at the resort are open air to allow cooling sea breezes.

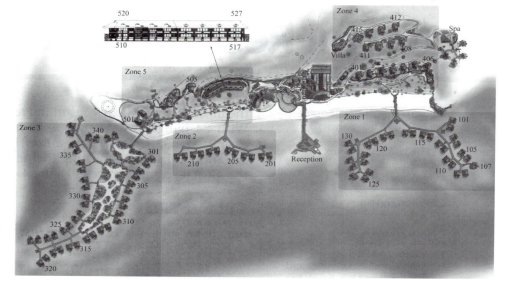

Figure 4.4.2   Plan of the resort (courtesy of Bora Bora Nui Resort & Spa).

Boutiques & Services

- Mandara Spa offers an extensive menu of spa treatments and services as well as four exquisite private bungalows each with its own jacuzzi, bathroom and massage table and a breathtaking view of Bora Bora
- Fully equipped fitness center
- Infinity swimming pool
- Private meeting room for up to 80 seated persons

- Over-water reception, set above a natural aquarium
- Laundry
- Dry cleaning service [...]
- Gift Boutique – Art Gallery
- Exclusive Black Pearl Boutique 'Robert Wan Company'
- Beauty salon with manicure and pedicure
- Helipad for Tours and Private transfers
- Boat transfer between the airport and resort
- Shuttle boat service for Vaitape Village [...]

Figure 4.4.3   View of the resort from the sea.

Figures 4.4.4–5   Pathways and boardwalks are used by both pedestrians and light maintenance vehicles.

Figure 4.4.6   The 600 m long artificial beach was built with sand dredged from the atoll's shipping channel.

Figures 4.5.10–11 Room height allows for vertical air movement and sensible cooling through stack effect ventilation making the indoor environment thermally comfortable.

Figure 4.5.12   The two parts of the resort – the guest unit one (on the left) and restaurant/office (on the right) – are separated, which, together with background noise from the breaking waves, ensures favourable acoustic conditions.

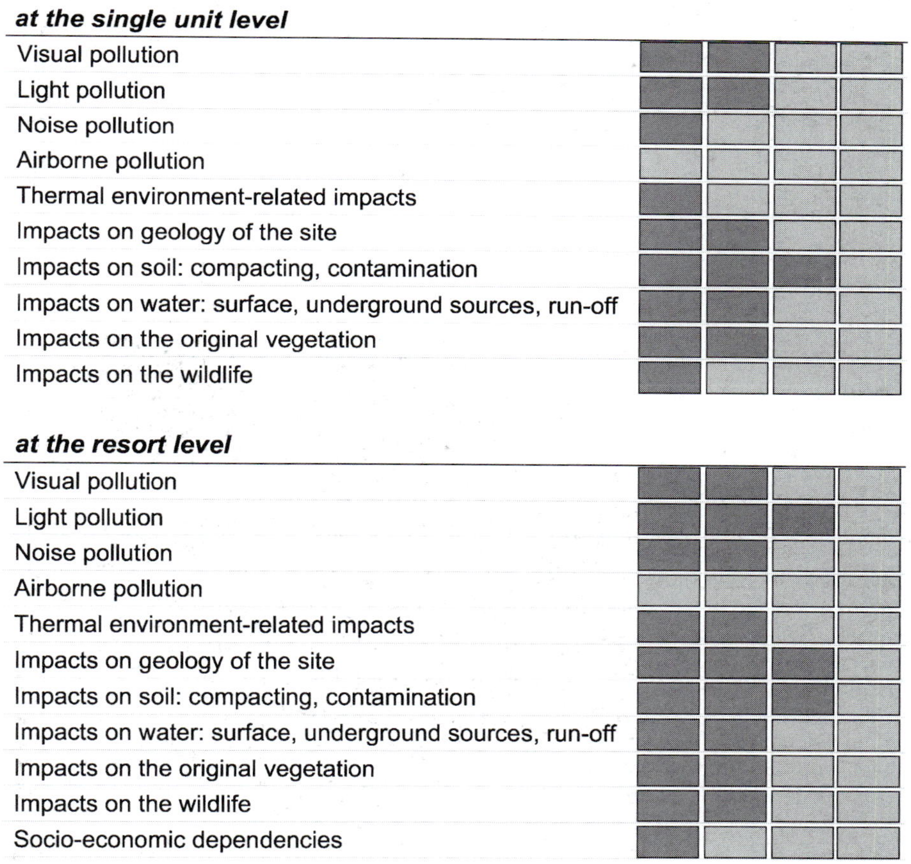

at the single unit level

Visual pollution				
Light pollution				
Noise pollution				
Airborne pollution				
Thermal environment-related impacts				
Impacts on geology of the site				
Impacts on soil: compacting, contamination				
Impacts on water: surface, underground sources, run-off				
Impacts on the original vegetation				
Impacts on the wildlife				

at the resort level

Visual pollution				
Light pollution				
Noise pollution				
Airborne pollution				
Thermal environment-related impacts				
Impacts on geology of the site				
Impacts on soil: compacting, contamination				
Impacts on water: surface, underground sources, run-off				
Impacts on the original vegetation				
Impacts on the wildlife				
Socio-economic dependencies				

Figure 4.5.13   The extent of the resort's potential environmental impacts. (**Note:** The extent of the resort's impacts [ranging from positive through neutral to negative] should be read in conjunction with the information in Figure 4.1).

temperatures (with fans switched off) were in the range 21.3–27.6 °C. This indicates quite efficient thermal design and some heat storage in massive elements of the structure (walls and floors). Conditions inside were quite similar to those outside in the shade and the range of indoor temperatures was a modified (dampened) reflection of the temperatures outdoors due to the 'mass effect' (Figures 4.5.8–9, Figures 4.5.10–11).

4.5.8 Concluding remarks

The resort's architecture is a variation of traditional Mexican themes with its white slightly sloping walls and small grilled openings. The heavyweight structure performs remarkably well in cooler conditions but it should respond equally well to the hot weather due to its unique double-storey open interior. The openness allows the warm air to move up beyond occupied height. A dominating colour scheme of white and blue, together with smooth tiled floors, psychologically reinforces the cooling effect achieved in this free-running building. Prudent energy and water management is also commendable (Figure 4.5.12, Figure 4.5.13).

4.6
Balamku Inn on the Beach

Location: Bahía Permejo, Mahahual, Quintana Roo, Mexico
Year of completion: 2006
Total cost of construction: US$550 K+ (approx.), owner-built (no add-on costs)
Architect/designer: Alan Knight and Carol Tumber
Consultant: Dinah Drago
Builder: Alan Knight with local craftspeople
Number of guest units: 4 double and 2 single storey units
Maximum number of guests: 30
Other facilities on site: reception, breakfast screened-in porch bar, lounge, office, gift shop, owners' accommodation, *palapa* (roofed patio), *bodega* (storage and accommodation), water tank, wind tower, battery room
Site area: 4 acres (1.6 ha)
Access methods: by road (from Cancún International airport, Chetumal airport or Mahahual harbour)
Principal attractions in the area: Costa Maya, Chínchorro reef, the lagoon and beach, Sian Ka'an World Biosphere Reserve, archaeological sites, nature and culture tours

4.6.1 In their own words

Balamku's Mission Statement and Explanation of Ecological Sustainability Practices

Balamku is committed to providing comfort and quality services using the resources of nature without abusing the environment (Figure 4.6.1).

We believe that we have an obligation to protect the environment and reduce the impact of tourism by using eco-efficient energy and water systems, waste management practices and preserving the natural environment.

Energy

All of our energy is provided by one of the largest solar panel installations on the Costa Maya. Wind generation has been added to complement this solar system. Consequently, we supply you with 24-hour electricity without a generator pounding away in the background. For those of you who have visited

Figure 4.6.1 Balamku Inn comprises guest units housed in single- and double-storey buildings.

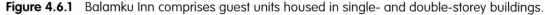

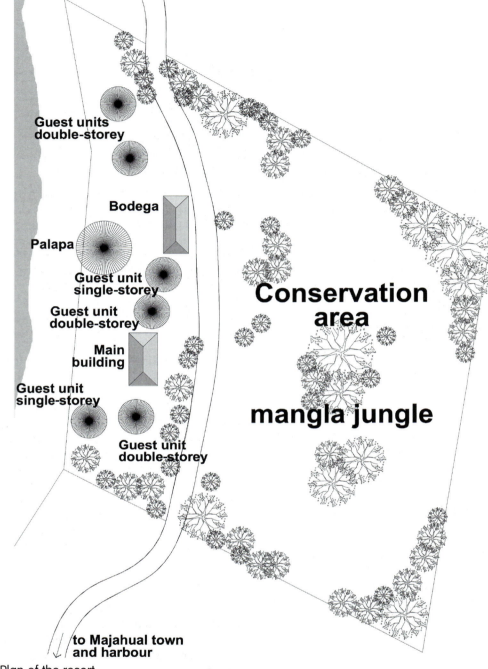

Figure 4.6.2 Plan of the resort.

this part of the world before, you will realize that this is quite a luxury. In return, we request you do not use energy-hungry appliances such as hairdryers (over 99 watts) and remember to turn off all lights and fans when they are not needed. All of our lights are energy efficient and the coffee-makers are low wattage.

In case mother nature fails, we have a quiet, propane (clean) back-up generator, but we are doing all possible to limit our need for it.

Figure 4.6.3 The largest building contains the reception, resort dining room and kitchen, with the office and owner/operator accommodation on the upper floor.

Water management

The water in the shower and sink is very clean (a mix of purchased city water and rainwater) but is not potable. Please use the bottled water for brushing your teeth, drinking and making coffee or tea. Every day we will refill your bottles with drinking water, which will limit the plastic refuse. If you need more, please help yourself to the water in the restaurant.

All the water from your shower and sink supports a constructed wetland located at the back of your building. As the water is supplying nutrients to the plants, we would be pleased if you used the environmental soap and shampoo provided in your bathroom.

Toilets

These water-saving toilets are easy to use. If you need more water, as you sit, lift the lever and count to 5; then, to flush, push the lever down very gently. As the waste is all composted, please don't put anything other than toilet paper down the toilet. If you have problems with the lever, please let us know as it is somewhat fragile.

Water usage with these toilets is reduced from a normal gallon [3.8l] a flush to one pint [0.5l].

In the future, we will be installing a system to purify our well water. Imagine a freshwater table just metres beneath the sand and so close to the sea. This gift could be compromised if septic tanks leak, and many do. Therefore, we have installed composting units at the back of each unit to manage the water and solid waste from the toilets. This system was designed by a biologist from Puerto Morales who recognized, as a diver, the sad reality of waste leaking into the sea and destroying the coral reef.

Recycling

All bottles and plastics are separated from other waste to assist in recycling. Organics from food preparation is composted in the bins behind the kitchen.

Water is available for refilling bottles to reduce the need for a new plastic bottle every day. Only new clients receive a new, unopened bottle. Towels and linens are changed every 2–3 days to reduce the water consumption.

Property management

The planning design of Balamku considered the protection of the many local species of trees and plants. The units are situated to maximize natural ventilation. The beach has a beautiful

Figures 4.6.4–5   Second-storey units benefit from high cathedral ceilings allowing hot air to rise under the roof; ground floor units have their thermal environment shaped by the openness of the plan and staying permanently in the 'shade' of the upper floor.

stone wall to reduce the risk of erosion. Vines and shrubs have intentionally been left to assist in further reduction of soil erosion as well as for the enjoyment of their natural beauty. We are continuously planting local trees and shrubs as well as sugar cane, banana, mango, papaya, and lime trees.

We would be very pleased to give you a brief tour of our systems [Source: Balamku Inn] (Figure 4.6.2).

of creating a wildlife refuge. Re-vegetation has been done with indigenous flowering plants but otherwise the landscaping scale has been quite modest. An attempt has been made to stop continuing beach erosion. In hindsight, the owners believe that the resort could do better with fewer buildings and lighter use of the land but with more vegetation (Figure 4.6.3, Figures 4.6.4–5).

4.6.2 Site selection and landscaping

The management has worked to preserve the original vegetation on the site. Nearly a third of the site remains undeveloped and a reforestation project has been undertaken with the aim

4.6.3 Construction

The resort is built chiefly with heavy materials such as concrete blocks and concrete laid in-situ as well as ceramic floor tiles. Materials require minimal maintenance and are resistant to strong

Figure 4.6.6 The resort's dining room has substantial thermal mass and stays comfortably cool even in hot weather conditions.

winds, thus increasing the structures' stability and safety in the hurricane season. Double-storey buildings also have tiled concrete floors between storeys. Local grass and timber are used for roofing allowing for sufficient heat dissipation into the night sky. Many resort activities take place outdoors in a traditional open-air structure called a *palapa*, which has no walls and only a light-weight grass roof supported by timber poles (Figure 4.6.6).

4.6.4 Energy management

Forty typical photovoltaic panels, each 0.5 by 1.5 m, provide the source of electricity. The daily gains are stored in a bank of 32 batteries. The PV panel-generated power meets about three-quarters of the total demand, the remainder coming from a wind turbine and a propane 11 kW back-up generator. Efficient low-voltage lighting and gas appliances, for example instantaneous gas water heaters, help to save energy. Landscape lighting is light sensor-operated. There are only a limited number of appliances drawing energy. The resort management appeals to guests to save energy in order to curb demand (Figure 4.6.7, Figure 4.6.8).

Figure 4.6.7 A 'mosquito magnet', which attracts and captures mosquitoes, helps to control the insect problem on site.

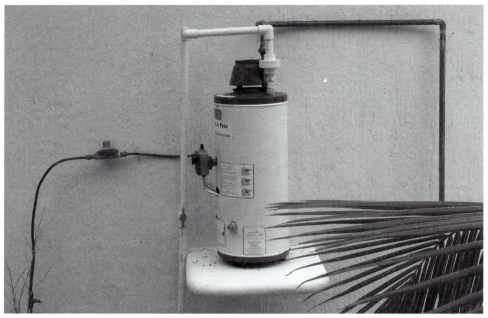

Figure 4.6.8 Small on-demand hot water heater.

Figure 4.6.9 Positioning a holding tank on the roof provides gravity, thus pressurising the system.

Figure 4.6.10 Each building has its own composting toilet unit.

Figure 4.6.11 The created wetlands are used for purifying grey water from sinks and showers.

Figure 4.6.12 Rooms are decorated with work by local artisans.

4.6.5 Water management

Mixing rainwater, collected in 170 000-litre cement cisterns, with water brought in by trucks covers the resort's water needs. On average, the resort uses 100 litres of water per day for every guest, which includes cooking needs. Water for direct human consumption is brought to the resort in large plastic containers and locally bottled or distributed from the containers. Water for irrigation is provided from a well and supplemented by recycled grey water from showers and sinks. All toilets are special extra-low flush systems and virtually all liquid waste is processed on site and recycled in created wetlands. Toilet water is filtered into a tank for use on large plants. There are plans for expanded utilisation of well water on site and for enlarging the leach fields (Figure 4.6.9).

4.6.6 Waste management

A local contractor takes most solid waste away to a communal landfill. Plastic, glass and metal waste is separated for collection and organic waste from the kitchen is composted. The liquid waste is processed on site in the resort's own sewage purifying system (constructed wetlands). There is a waste

Figures 4.6.13–14   Resort buildings are built relatively close to each other leaving a large tract of land reserved for the resort's conservation effort.

reduction strategy in place that applies to plastic bottles. Bulk purchases of water and toiletries, soap and shampoo dispensers rather than single-use individual containers, and encouragement given to reuse and recycling further reduce waste generation (Figure 4.6.10, Figure 4.6.11).

4.6.7 The resort's climatic performance

During the visit to the resort in early December (early 'winter'), external temperatures ranged from 22.9–26.4 °C and corresponding internal temperatures (with fans switched off) were in the range 24.6–27.4 °C. This indicates quite significant heat storage in massive elements (structural walls and

floors) of the resort. Conditions inside were slightly warmer than those outside in the corresponding period and the range of indoor temperatures also was small. One would expect the performance to be equally good in warmer months (Figure 4.6.12).

4.6.8 Concluding remarks

The heavyweight structure design employs a strategy that relies on thermal mass for comfort. All ground floor rooms have concrete floors coupled to the ground for cooling, massive concrete walls to slow down heat flows, and they are also well shaded by the upper floor. The upstairs rooms, on the other hand, have high cathedral ceilings and lightweight

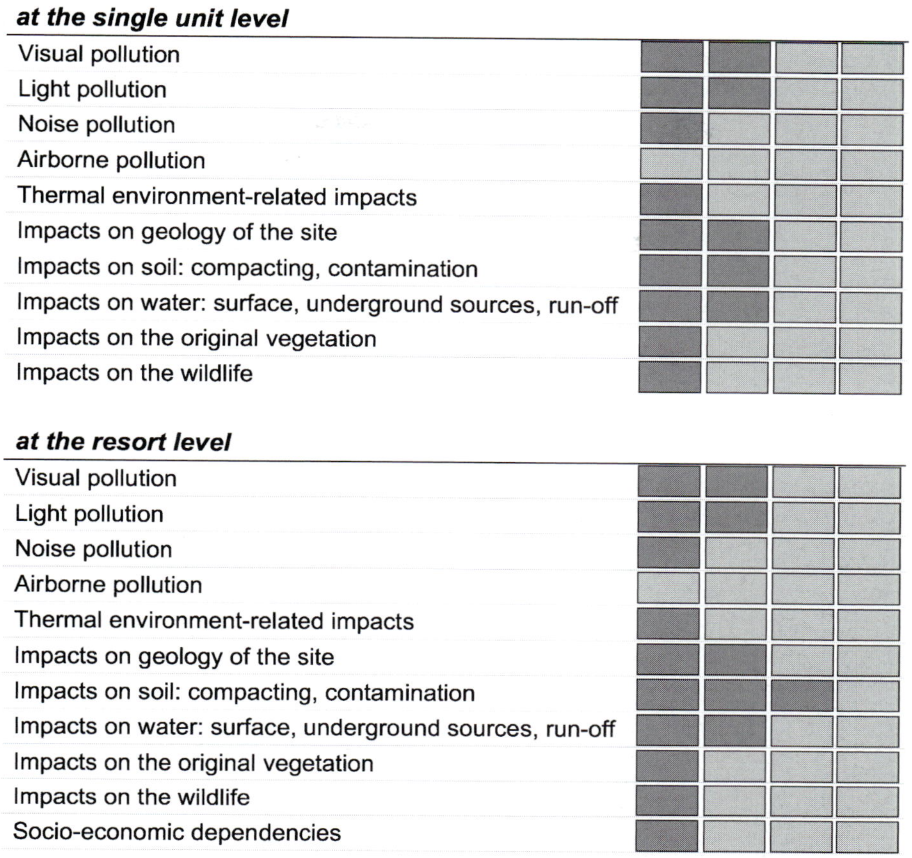

at the single unit level

Visual pollution
Light pollution
Noise pollution
Airborne pollution
Thermal environment-related impacts
Impacts on geology of the site
Impacts on soil: compacting, contamination
Impacts on water: surface, underground sources, run-off
Impacts on the original vegetation
Impacts on the wildlife

at the resort level

Visual pollution
Light pollution
Noise pollution
Airborne pollution
Thermal environment-related impacts
Impacts on geology of the site
Impacts on soil: compacting, contamination
Impacts on water: surface, underground sources, run-off
Impacts on the original vegetation
Impacts on the wildlife
Socio-economic dependencies

Figure 4.6.15   The extent of the resort's potential environmental impacts. (**Note:** The extent of resort's impacts [ranging from positive through neutral to negative] should be read in conjunction with the information in Figure 4.1).

roofs fast dissipating any heat build-ups. Unit walls, built on a circular plan, present only a small section perpendicular to the direction of the sun's rays and, being painted white, reflect a lot of incident solar radiation.

The owner/operator's ambition is to provide environmental education by exemplary environmental practices. The emphasis is on a concerted conservation effort and the resort is a leader in the area in this regard (Figures 4.6.13–14, Figure 4.6.15).

4.7
KaiLuumcito the Camptel

Location:	Rio Indio beach, Mahahual, Quintana Roo, Mexico
Year of completion:	2001
Total cost of construction:	US$110 K+ (approx.), owner-built (no add-on costs)
Architect/designer:	Clayton Ball
Consultant:	Arnold Bilgore
Builder:	local craftspeople
Number of guest units:	17 *tentalapas* (tent units)
Max. number of guests:	40 (approx.)
Other facilities on site:	*palapa* containing lounge, dining and kitchen, four staff units, two bath and toilet blocks, battery room
Site area:	5.45 acres (2.18 ha)
Access methods:	by road (from Cancún international airport, Chetumal airport or Mahahual harbour)
Principal attractions in the area:	Costa Maya, Chínchorro reef, the lagoon and beach, Sian Ka'an World Biosphere Reserve, archaeological sites, nature and culture tours

4.7.1 Site selection and landscaping

The principal reason for selecting this particular site was acquisition of exclusive rights of access to an inland lagoon, which is a nature reserve and a bird sanctuary. A small jetty for launching kayaks was built and a narrow path, leading through the jungle to the lagoon, was laid out (Figure 4.7.1).

The 'camptel' brings very little disturbance to the original farm site. A concrete slab has been removed and some native vegetation has been planted to improve visual privacy (Figure 4.7.2).

4.7.2 Construction

The resort is built chiefly with light and natural raw materials such as timber poles, grass or palm-leaf thatch and tent fabric. The conditions 'indoors' thus offered, very closely resemble those found in the

Figure 4.7.1 The super-low weight of KaiLuumcito structures allows them to sit right on the beach.

Figure 4.7.2   The main reason for bringing the resort to its current site was the natural lagoon and its wildlife.

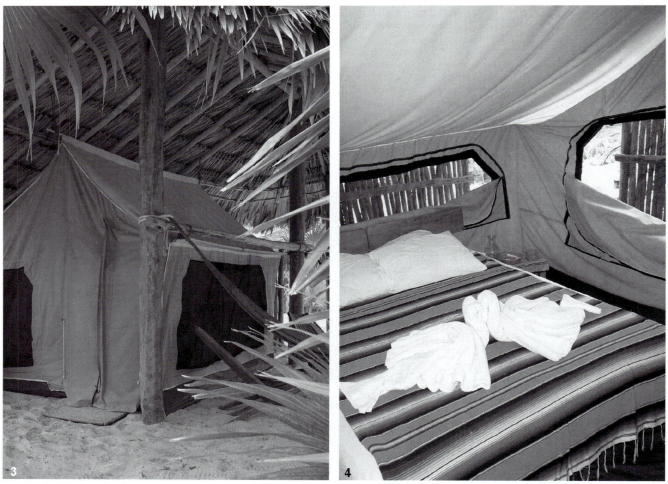

Figures 4.7.3–4   The KaiLuumcito accommodation is provided in *tentalapas* – a combination of specially designed tents shaded by *palapas* (traditional Mexican roofed structures without walls).

Figures 4.7.5–6   The resort structures have been erected using traditional local building techniques and the expertise of the local labour force.

Figure 4.7.7   The resort's lounge in the main *palapa* has walls made with sticks arranged to provide visual privacy of the area.

Figures 4.7.8–9   Toilet blocks are rather conventional except for lighting, which comes from oil lamps; washing rooms are external parts of the toilet block entirely open to the air.

Figure 4.7.10   Diesel torches are lit at dusk and provide lighting until fuel burns out.

Figure 4.7.11 All structures at the resort utilise natural materials in their simplest unprocessed form.

shade outdoors. *Tentalapas*, which are tents erected under shading thatched *palapa* roofs, offer shelter from rain and wind but do not resist heat flows (Figures 4.7.3–4, Figures 4.7.5–6, Figure 4.7.7).

4.7.3 Energy management

There is no electricity used at the resort other than that coming from a single 75 W solar panel. In the kitchen, a propane stove, two ovens and a refrigerator are used, burning around 480 litres of propane per year. A gas heater also heats hot water for the kitchen.

Lighting (including lighting of the area) is provided with diesel torches and candles, however a move to solar lighting is under consideration (Figures 4.7.8–9, Figure 4.7.10).

4.7.4 Water management

The resort's own well delivers 375 litres per day. Rainwater is also harvested during the wet season from September to October and collected in a 57 000-litre tank. This water is filtered and mixed with the water trucked in (approximately 10 000 litres per

Figure 4.7.12   General view of the KaiLuumcito shows both toilet blocks and a file of tentalapas along the beach.

Figures 4.7.13–14   Both the kitchen and the dining hall are housed in the main *palapa* of the resort; neither room has walls.

Figure 4.7.15   The history of KaiLuumcito commenced in 1976; the resort has been devastated several times by major cyclones and has required rebuilding.

fortnight), to yield 145 litres per guest per day. Most of the water is used by divers for showering and washing their equipment (diving is the principal activity attraction offered by the resort) (Figure 4.7.11).

4.7.5 Waste management

A contractor takes most solid waste away to a local landfill. Plastic, glass and metal waste is recycled. Organic waste from the kitchen is taken away for composting by locals. The liquid waste is processed on site in a septic system connected to a leach field (solids are carted away every six months). The operators plan installation of ecological mulching toilets. Buying in bulk reduces unnecessary packaging waste (Figure 4.7.12).

4.7.6 The resort's climatic performance

During a visit to the resort early in December (early 'winter'), external temperatures ranged from

Figure 4.8.6 Al fresco dining is offered at the main house of the Hacienda, which was built for its Spanish owners in the eighteenth century.

local contractor takes most solid waste away to a municipal landfill. Plastic, glass and metal waste is recycled. Organic waste from the kitchen is composted on site or taken away by employees for that purpose (Figure 4.8.7).

4.8.6 The resort's climatic performance

During the author's visit to the resort early in December (early 'winter'), external temperatures ranged from 23.9–29.9 °C and corresponding internal temperatures (with fans switched off) were in the range 26.0–30.1 °C. This indicates quite significant heat storage in massive elements (structural walls and floors) of the resort. Conditions inside were

Figure 4.8.7 The change of character from a former cattle ranch to a tourist resort is most visible in the landscaping design; view from the restaurant deck towards one of the accommodation buildings.

warmer than those outside for the corresponding period and the range of indoor temperatures was fairly small. It can be predicted, with some level of certainty, that in warmer weather the indoors will offer an environment quite a lot cooler than on the outside. Lack of sufficient natural ventilation seems problematic but this could easily be resolved with low-powered exhaust fans installed near the highest points of the ceiling. The roofs, which are quite flat, would probably benefit from more insulation but, being reasonably well shaded by palm trees, this overlooked aspect does not cause the buildings to perform significantly worse (Figure 4.8.8).

4.8.7 Concluding remarks

The Ancient Maya were intimately connected with the natural balance of the environment and the resort's current operators are committed to restore

Figure 4.8.8 The Hacienda has undertaken a massive effort of re-vegetating degraded parts of the property with indigenous plants, giving employment to the local villagers in the process.

Figure 4.8.9 The property has its own historic attractions including a small church built by the Spaniards in the seventeenth century.

this tradition in today's Maya rural society around the Hacienda. The resort's spa, the Yaxkin Maya Retreat, offers guests a unique opportunity to experience some of the most healing organic traditions known today that are rooted in holistic Maya ceremonies and rituals. An old natural cave – the *rejoyada* or dried *cenote* (sinkhole) near the main gardens overlooking the nunnery and other Mayan temples – has been rescued for that purpose. The place was used in ancient times as an underground ritual cave and more recently (in the 1920s) as a storage site.

The resort's site is known also as 'Yaxkin', which means 'the place of renewal' and, as part of its mission, a percentage of its profits will be donated to the environmental protection and animal welfare efforts of the Maya Nature Conservation programme. This programme has already reforested the area with over 2000 native hardwood trees and has vigilantly kept out illegal hunting of endangered animal species, such as the kinkajou, in the area. Work has also started on a *zumpul-che* (a sacred Maya sweat-bath similar to the Aztec's *temazcal*) to help regain understanding of the important relationship between steam (water) and heat (fire) to purify the spirit, mind and body to balance the inner energy flow or life force in us.

Another important part of the resort is the Merle Greene Gallery which has over 20 large 'rubbings' from her personal collection, donated to support the resort's commitment to continue fomenting the study and acknowledgement of ancient Maya cultural heritage in the region.

Baggs, S., and Baggs, J. (1996) *The healthy house*. HarperCollins Publishers.

Baker, N.V. (1993) Comfort in passive buildings. *Proceedings of the CEC symposium 'Solar energy and buildings'*. Athens, 8–10 December 1993.

Baker, N.V. editor. (1987) *Passive and low energy design for tropical island climates*. Commonwealth Secretariat, London.

Balcomb, J.D. (1993) Integrated design. *Proceedings of the CEC symposium Solar energy and buildings*. Athens, 8–10 December 1993.

Balcomb, J.D. editor. (1992) *Passive solar buildings*. The MIT Press, Cambridge, Mass.

Balcomb, J.D., Jones, R.J., Kosiewicz, C.E., Lazarus, G.S., McFarland, R.D., and Wray, W.O. (1984) *Passive solar design handbook*. American 'Solar Design Society', New York.

Balcomb, J.D., Barley, C.D., McFarland, R.D., Perry, J.E. Jr., Wray, W.O., and Noll, S. (1980) *Passive Solar Design Handbook*, **2**. DOE/CS-0127/2. US Department of Energy, Washington, DC.

Ballinger, J.A., Prasad, D.K., and Rudder, D. (1992) *Energy efficient Australian housing*. 2nd edn, Australian Government Publishing Service, Canberra.

Baud-Bovy, M., and Lawson, F. (1977) *Tourism and recreation development*. Architectural Press, London.

Baud-Bovy, M., and Lawson, F. (1998) *Tourism and recreation handbook of planning and design*. Architectural Press, London.

Baum, C. (2007) Back to nature. *Mercedes Magazine Australia*, Winter/Spring, pp. 64–65.

Baverstock, G., and Paolino, S. (1986) *Low energy buildings in Australia* **1**: Graphic Systems, Perth.

Baverstock, G.F., D'Cruz, N., and Healey, J. (1992) Energy efficiency of new generation solar buildings can save 60% to 90% of the energy demand compared with conventional buildings. *Proceedings of the 26th ANZAScA Conference*. Perth, 6–10 July 1992.

Beer, A.R. (1990) *Environmental planning for site development*. E & NF Spon, London.

Bell, S. (1994) *Visual landscape design*. British Forestry Commission and the Ministry of Forests, BC.

Bennetts, H., Williamson, T., and Coldicutt, S. (1994) Floors in the argument. *Proceedings of the 28th ANZAScA Conference*. Geelong, 26–28 September 1994, pp. 15–20.

Best practice eco-tourism: a guide to energy and waste minimization (1997). Office of National Tourism, Canberra.

Birkeland, J. (2002) *Design for sustainability: a sourcebook of integrated eco-logical solutions*. Earthscan Publications, London.

Birmingham, J. (1995) What on Earth is ecotourism? *Escape Issue* 3, p. 20.

Boele, N. (1996) *Sustainable Energy Technologies for the Australian Tourism Industry*. Tourism Council Australia, Barton, ACT.

Brand, S. (1994) *How buildings learn*. Viking, London.

Bromberek, Z. (1995) *Passive climate control for tourist facilities in the coastal tropics (Far North Queensland)* (PhD thesis), Department of Architecture, University of Queensland, Brisbane.

Bromberek, Z. (1999) Tourists and attitudes to air-conditioning. *Climate Research* **13**: 141–147.

Bromberek, Z. (2002a) Sustainability, architecture and comfort: a biotechnological model of environmental adaptation. *Proceedings of the Sustainable Building 2002 Conference*. Oslo, Norway, 23–25 September 2002, CD-ROM.

Bromberek, Z. (2002b) Eco-tourism and comfort in the tropics. *Proceedings of the International Symposium Oxford Brookes University, UK and University of Tarumanagara*. Jakarta, Indonesia, 14–16 October 2002, pp. 155–170.

Bromberek, Z. (2006) Tropical tourist resorts and air-conditioning. In *Challenges for architectural science in changing climate* (S. Shannon, Vl Soebarto and T. Williamson, eds) Proceedings of the 40th ANZAScA Annual Conference 22–25 November 2006, Adelaide University, Adelaide.

Brown, S. (2005) *The feng shui bible*. Godsfield Press, London.

Brown, G.Z., and DeKay, M. (2001) *Sun, wind and light: architectural design strategies*. 2nd edn, John Wiley & Sons.

Brown, G.Z., Haglund, B., Loveland, J., Reynolds, J., and Ubbelohde, M.S. (1992) *Insideout: design procedures for passive environmental technologies*. 2nd edn, John Wiley & Sons, New York.

Building energy manual (1993) NSW Public Works, Sydney.

Bulletin 8: Sunshine and shade in Australasia 5th edn. National Building Technology Centre, Chatswood, NSW.

Burberry, P. (1992) *Environment and services*. 7th edn, Longman Scientific & Technical, UK.

Burberry, P. (1978) *Building for energy conservation*. Architectural Press, London.

Carabateas, E.N. (1993) Research objectives and trends. *Proceedings of the CEC symposium 'Solar energy and buildings'*. Athens, 8–10 December 1993.

Carbon Trust (2005a) *Supporting tomorrow's low carbon technologies*. The Carbon Trust, London.

Carbon Trust (2005b) *The Carbon Trust's Small-Scale CHP field trial update*. The Carbon Trust, London.

Carruthers, D.D. (1991) The matching of house design to climate. *Proceedings of the 25th ANZAScA Conference*. Adelaide 15–19 July 1991, pp. 87–91.

Cavanaugh, W.J., and Wilkes, J.A. (1999) *Architectural Acoustics: Principles and Practice*. John Wiley & Sons, New York.

Ceballos-Lascuráin, H. (1996) *Tourism, ecotourism, and protected areas: the state of nature-based tourism around the world and guidelines for its development*, Gland, Switz.: The International Union for the Conservation of Nature (IUCN).

CIBS Guide A1. Environmental criteria for design (1978) Chartered Institution of Building Services, London.

CIBS Guide A5. Thermal response of buildings (1979) Chartered Institution of Building Services, London.

Clark, B.D. (1994) Improving public participation in environmental impact assessment. *Built Environment* **20**(4)(4): **294–308.**

Clarke, J.A. (1993) Building performance modelling. *Proceedings of the CEC symposium 'Solar energy and buildings'*. Athens, 8–10 December 1993.

Climate of Australia (1989) Bureau of Meteorology, Canberra.

Climate and house design **1**: Design of low-cost housing and community facilities (1971) UN, New York.

Climatic averages Australia (1975) Australian Government Publishing Service, Canberra.

Commercial Building Incentive Program (1999) Technical Guide Hotels/Motels Office of Energy Efficiency, Ottawa.

Conway, M., and Liston, L.L. (1990) *The weather handbook*. Conway Data, Atlanta.

Cooper, C. (1992) The life cycle concept and strategic planning for coastal resorts. *Built Environment* **18**(1)(1): **57–66.**

Correa, C. (1994) An architecture for Mauritius. *Proceedings of the Commonwealth Association of Architects Conference*. Mauritius, 22–28 May 1994.

Cowan, H.J. editor. (1980) *Solar energy applications in the design of buildings*. Applied Science Publishers, London.

Cox, G.B. (1993) Thermal performance of housing in North Queensland (thesis), University of Queensland, Brisbane.

Critchfield, H.J. (1983) *General climatology*. 4th edn, Prentice Hall, Englewood Cliffs, NJ.

Crosbie, M.J. (1994) *Green architecture: a guide to sustainable design*. Rockport Publishers, Mass.

Crowden, G.P. (1953) Indoor climate and thermal comfort in the tropics. *Proceedings of the Conference on Tropical Architecture*. University College, London 24 March 1953, pp. 27–35.

Crowther, R.L. (1977) *Sun/Earth: how to apply free energy sources to our homes and buildings*. Crowther/Solar Group, Denver, Col.

Crowther, R.L. (1992) *Ecologic architecture*. Butterworth Architecture, Boston.

Croy, W.G., and Høgh, L. (2002) Endangered visitors: a phenomenological study of eco-resort development. *Current Issues in Tourism* **5**(3 & 4).

Cullen, P. (1978) The development of environmental impact statements. In: McMaster, J.C., and Webb, G.R. editors., *Australian project evaluation*. Australia & New Zealand Book Co, Sydney.

Daly, H.E. (1992) Steady state economics: concepts, questions, and politics. *Ecological Economics*, pp. 333–338.

Danby, M. (1963) *Grammar of architectural design with special reference to the tropics*. Oxford University Press, London.

Dawson, A. (2000) Are architects able to address the issues in the design of sustainable buildings? Keynote address in the *Proceedings of the 34th Conference of the Australian and New Zealand Architectural Science Association* 1–3 December, Adelaide University, Adelaide, pp. 1–7.

Day, C. (2004) *Places of the soul: architecture and environmental design as a healing art*. Architectural Press, Oxford.

de Dear, R.J. (1994) Outdoor climatic influences on indoor thermal comfort requirements. *Proceedings of the Building Research Establishment '93 conference*, Garston, Watford, UK, pp. 107–133.

de Dear, R., Fountain, M., Popovic, S., Watkins, S., Brager, G., Arens, E., and Benton, C. (1993) *A field study of occupant comfort and office thermal environments in a hot–humid climate. Final report RP–702*. American Society of Heating, Refrigerating and Air-Conditioning Engineers.

Department for Education and Skills (2003) *Sustainability Development Report*, DES, UK.

Department of Housing and Works (2002) *Sustainability and the built environment*. A submission to the State Sustainability Strategy Department of Housing and Works, GWA, Perth.

DES see Department for Education and Skills.

DHW see Department of Housing and Works.

Docherty, M., and Szokolay, S.V. (1999) *Climate analysis. PLEA Note 5*. Passive and Low Energy Architecture International, Brisbane.

Dohrmann, D.R., and Alereza, T. (1993) Analysis of survey data on HVAC maintenance costs. *ASHRAE Journal* RP No. 3012, pp. 550–564.

Drumm, A., Moore, A., Soles, A., Patterson, C., and Terborgh, J.E. (2004) *Ecotourism Development – A Manual for Conservation Planners and Managers*. **II**: The Business of Ecotourism Development and Management, The Nature Conservancy, Arlington, VA.

Drysdale, J.W. (1975) *Designing houses for Australian climates*. 3rd edn, AGPS, Canberra.

Dutton, G. (1986) *The book of Australian islands*. Macmillan, Sydney.

Eagles, P.F. (1995) Understanding the market for sustainable tourism. In *Linking tourism, the environment, and sustainability* (S.F. McCool and A.E. Watson, eds) pp., US Department of Agriculture, pp. 25–33.

Eagles, P.F., and McCool, J. (2002) *Tourism in national parks and protected areas: planning and management*. CABI Publishing, Wallingford.

Ecolodges: exploring opportunities for sustainable business. (2004) International Finance Corporation, Washington, DC.

Ecotourism: adding value to tourism in natural areas. A discussion paper on nature-based tourism (1994) Department of Tourism, Sport and Recreation, Hobart.

Egan, M.D. (1983) *Concepts in architectural lighting*. McGraw-Hill Book Company.

Ellen, C. (1985) Thermal performance of roofs. *BCME* August/September, pp. 42–47.

English, P.W., and Mayfield, R.C. editors. (1972) *Man, space, and environment*. Oxford University Press, New York.

Environmental Tourism Audit–how we are tracking, (2000) *Tourism Queensland News* No. 1, p. 12.

Evans, M., McDonagh, P., and Moutinho, L. (1992) The coastal hotel sector: performance and perception analysis. *Built Environment* **18**(1)(1): **67–78.**

Evans, M. (1980) *Housing, climate and comfort*. Architectural Press, London.

Fanger, P.O. (1970) *Thermal comfort*. Danish Technical Press, Copenhagen.

Fanger, P.O. (1973) The influence of age, sex, adaptation, season and circadian rhythm on thermal comfort criteria for man. *Proceedings of L'Institute Internacional du Froid's meeting Vienna*.

FEMP see Federal Energy Management Program in Internet sources section below.

Fisher T.A. (1992) Five principles of environmental architecture, AIA, New York.

Flannery, T. (1995) *Future eaters*. George Braziller, Sydney.

Florida Solar Energy Center (1981–1997) *Design notes. Concepts in passive design*. FSEC, Cocoa, Flo.

Florida Solar Energy Center (1984) *Principles of low energy building design in warm humid climates*. FSEC, Cape Canaveral, Flo.

Fordham, M., and Partners. (1999) *Environmental Design: An Introduction for Architects and Engineers*. 2nd edn, Spon Press, London.

Forwood, B.S.A. (1980) The use of computers for modelling the physical environments in buildings. In: Cowan, H.J. editor. *Solar energy applications in the design of buildings*. Applied Science Publishers, London pp. 143–169.

Forwood, B.S.A. (1995) Redefining the concept of thermal comfort for naturally ventilated buildings. *Proceedings of the 29th ANZAScA Conference*. Canberra, 11–13 July 1995.

Fountain, M., Brager, G., Arens, E., Bauman, F., and Benton, C. (1997) Comfort control for short-term occupancy. *Energy and Buildings* **21**(1)(1): **1–13.**

Fraenkel, P. (1979) *The power guide. A catalogue of small-scale power equipment*. Intermediate Technology Publications Ltd, London.

Freitas de, C.R. (1979) *Beach climate and recreation* (PhD thesis). Department of Architecture, University of Queensland, Brisbane.

French, J. and Sullivan, B. (1994) *Switch!: home-based power, water and sewage systems for the twenty-first century*. Aird Books, Flemington, Vic. Aus.

Future directions: sustainable tourism and land use scenarios for the Carnarvon-Ningalo coast (2003) Western Australian Planning Commission, Perth.

Future use of North West and Mast Head Islands (1973) Brisbane: Queensland Co-ordinator General's Department.

Gallo, C. ed. (1998) *Bioclimatic architecture*. Italian National Institute of Architecture.

Galloway, T. (2004) *Solar house: a guide for the solar designer*. Architectural Press, Oxford, UK.

Geiger, R. (1950) (1966: transl. from 4th edn) *The climate near the ground*. Harvard University Press, Cambridge, Mass.

Gertsakis, J., Lewis, H., and Ryan, C. (1997) *A guide to EcoReDesign*. RMIT Centre for Design, Melbourne.

Gibbs, W.J., Maher, J.V., and Coughlan, M.J. (1978) Climatic variability and extremes. In: Pittock, A.B., Frakes, L.A., Jenssen, D., Peterson, J.A., and Zillman, J.W. editors., *Climatic change and variability: a southern perspective*. Cambridge University Press, Cambridge.

Givoni, B. (1962) Basic study of ventilation problems in hot countries. Building Research Station, Haifa.

Givoni, B. (1976) *Man, climate and architecture*. 2nd edn, Van Nostrand Reinhold, New York.

Givoni, B. (1994) *Passive and low energy cooling of buildings*. Van Nostrand Reinhold, New York.

Givoni, B. (1998) *Climate considerations in building and urban design*. Van Nostrand Reinhold, New York.

Godwin, T. (1995) Bioclimatic architecture. *CAArchitect News Net*, First Quarter, p. 6.

Gokhale-Madan, M. (1994) Limitations of the envelope concept: the first threshold. *Proceedings of the 28th ANZAScA Conference*. Geelong, 26–28 September 1994, pp. 75–79.

Gokhale-Madan, M., and Hyde, R.A. (1993) Thermal performance of lightweight construction systems: a study in Queensland context. *Proceedings of the 27th ANZAScA Conference.* Sydney, 12–14 November 1993.

Good health in the tropics (1979) Australian Government Publishing Service, Canberra.

Goodall, B. (1992) Coastal resorts: development and redevelopment. *Built Environment* **18**(1)(1): **5–11.**

Gordon, I., and Goodall, B. (1992) Resort cycles and development process. *Built Environment* **18**(1)(1): **41–56.**

Goulding, J.R., Lewis, J.O., and Steemers, T.C. editors. (1992) *Energy conscious design.* Batsford for the Commission of the European Communities, London.

Goulding, J.R., Lewis, J.O., and Steemers, T.C. editors. (1992) *Energy in architecture: the European passive solar handbook.* Batsford for the Commission of the European Communities.

Gourlay, M. (1983) Accretion and erosion of coral cays and some consequent implications for the management of marine parks. In J.T. Baker, R.M. Carter, P.W. Sammarco and K.P. Stark, eds., *Proceedings of the Inaugural Great Barrier Reef Conference,* Townsville, James Cook University, 29 August–2 September, pp. 475–482.

Gourou, P. (1968) *The tropical world.* 4th edn, Longmans, London.

Greenland, J. (1993) *Foundation of architectural science.* 2nd edn, University of Technology, Sydney.

Greenland, J., and Szokolay, S. (1985) *Passive solar design in Australia.* RAIA, Canberra.

Gregory, J., and Darby, F. (1990). *Solar efficient design for housing.* Solar Energy Council, Melbourne.

Hall, D.C. (1990) Preliminary estimates of cumulative private and external costs of energy. *Contemporary Policy Issues* **viii**(3)(3): **283–307.**

Halley, K. (1992) The tourist accommodation market. *The Architecture Show,* September/October, pp. 26–27.

Hardy, A., and Beeton, R. (2001) Stakeholder perceptions of sustainable tourism: lessons learnt from a study in the Daintree Region of Far North Queensland, Australia. *Proceedings of the CAUTHE National Research Conference,* pp. 132–144.

Harris, N.P. (1987) A hedonist's handbook to full enjoyment of the elements – part one: housed in the Top End, Australia. In *Science and life in the tropics:* portfolio of papers presented at the 57th ANZAAS Congress, Townsville 24–28 August 1987.

Harris, C.M. (1994) *Noise control in buildings: a practical guide for architects and engineers.* McGraw-Hill, New York.

Hastings, S.R. editor. (1994) *Passive solar commercial and institutional buildings: a sourcebook of examples and design insights.* John Wiley & Sons.

Hawkes, D. (1996) *The Environmental Tradition: Studies In The Architecture Of Environment.* E & FN Spon, London.

Hollo, N. (1995) *Warm House Cool House.* Choice Books, Marrickville, NSW.

Holm, D. (1983) *Energy conservation in hot climates.* Architectural Press, London.

Hooper, C. (1975) *Design for climate. Guidelines for the design of low cost houses for the climates of Kenya.* Housing Research and Development Unit, University of Nairobi.

Houghton, J. (2004) *Global warming.* 3rd edn, Cambridge University Press, Cambridge.

Housing for life. Design for everybody (2001) Master Builders Association of the ACT.

Hulsher, W., and Fraenkel, P. (1994) *The power guide. An international catalogue of small-scale power equipment.* 2nd edn, Intermediate Technology Publications, London.

Humphreys, M.A. (1978) Outdoor temperatures and comfort indoors. *Building Research and Practice* **6**(2)(2): **92–105.**

Hyde, R. (2000) *Climate responsive design.* E & FN Spon, London.

IHVE Guide (1977-A3–7) *Thermal and other properties of building structures.* Chartered Institution of Building Services.

International Union of Architects (UIA) (1993) *Declaration of Interdependence for a Sustainable Future.* Union Internationale des Architectes, Chicago–Paris.

International Union for the Conservation of Nature and Natural Resources, World Conservation Union, United Nation Environment Programme, and World Wide Fund for Nature (1991) *Caring for the Earth* IUCN/UNEP/WWF: Gland, Switzerland.

Isles of the sun and Great Barrier Reef n.d. Queensland Government Tourist Bureau, Brisbane.

IUCN see International Union for the Conservation of Nature and Natural Resources.

Izmir, G. (1995) Being seen to be green. *Business-to-Business Review,* May, pp. 20–22.

Jones-Crabtree, A.J., Pearce, A.R., and Chen, V.C.P. (1998) Implementing sustainability knowledge into the built environment: an assessment of current approaches. *IERC Conference Proceedings.* 9–12 May 1998, Banff, BC, Canada, http://maven.gtri.gatech.edu/sfi/resources/pdf/cp/cp007.pdf.

Jones, D.L. (1998) *Architecture and the environment: bioclimatic building design.* The Overlook Press, NY.

Karyono, T.H. (1996) Thermal comfort in the tropical South East Asia region. *Architectural Science Review* **39**: 135–139.

Kay, M., Ballinger, J.A., Harris, S., and Hora, U. (1982) *Energy efficient site planning handbook*. Housing Commission of NSW, Sydney.

Kellog Smith, F., and Bertolone, F.J. (1986) *Bringing interiors to light*. Whitney Library of Design, NY.

Kempton, W. (1992) Introduction. *Energy and Buildings* **18**(2)(2): **171–176**.

Kevan, S.M. (1993) Quest for pleasurable cure: a history of tourism for climate and health. *Proceedings of the 13th International Congress of Biometeorology*. **2**. Calgary, pp. 615–623.

Khan, M.A. (1995) Concepts, definitions and key issues in sustainable development: the outlook for the future. *Proceedings of the International Sustainable Development Research Conference*. Manchester.

Khawaja, M., Potiowsky, T.P., and Peach, H.G. (1990) Cost–effectiveness of conservation programs: the Hood River experiment. *Contemporary Policy Issues* **viii**(3)(3): **174–184**.

King, E. (1995) *Africa's wild about tourism*. Good Weekend, Sydney, November 4, pp. 79–81.

Koenigsberger, O.H., Ingersoll, T.G., Mayhew, A., and Szokolay, S.V. (1973) *Manual of tropical housing and building. Part one: Climatic design*. Longmans, London and New York.

Konya, A. (1980) *Design primer for hot climates*. Architectural Press, London.

Kremers, J.A. (2000) *Defining sustainable architecture*. Architronic viewed 29/5/2000 <www.saed.kent.edu/architronic/v4n3/v4n3.02a.html>.

Kunz, M.N. editor. (2004) *Beach Hotels*. teNeues Publishing Group, New York.

Kurosawa, S. (1995) Oceania's happy isles set out to broaden your holiday horizons. *The Australian*, June 22, p. 17.

Lawson, F. (1995) *Hotels and resorts: planning, design and refurbishment*. Architectural Press, Oxford.

Lawson, B. (1996) *Building materials: energy and the environment*. RAIA, Canberra.

Lee, D.H.K., and Austin, H. (1963) *Evaluation of thermal environment in shelters*. US Department of Health, Education and Welfare, Cincinnati, PHS.

Lee, T., and Williamson, T.J. (1995) The Australian solar radiation data handbook – the third edition. *Proceedings of the 29th ANZAScA Conference*. Canberra, 11–13 July 1995, pp. 55–61.

Lewis, P.J. (1993) Defining and measuring the intensity of heat waves – incorporation of the humidity factor. *Proceedings of the 13th International Congress of Biometeorology*. **2**. Calgary, pp. 540–553.

Lima, M.A. (1994) Architectural science and the issues of regionalism and internationalism. *Proceedings of the 28th ANZAScA Conference*. Geelong, 26–28 September 1994, pp. 135–139.

Litter, J., and Randall, T. (1984) *Design with energy: The conservation and use of energy in buildings*. Cambridge University Press, Cambridge.

Llewellyn, P. (1999) Understanding energy efficiency. Part 2: Thermal mass versus lightweight timber construction. *Australian Timber Design*, summer, p. 20.

Loe, D., and Manfield, K.P. (1998) *Daylighting design in architecture: making the most of a natural resource*. BRECSU, Building Research Establishment Ltd, Garston.

Lomborg, B. (2001) *The skeptical environmentalist: measuring the real state of the world*. Cambridge University Press, Cambridge.

Lowry, W.P. (1991) *Atmospheric ecology for designers and planners*. Van Nostrand Reinhold, New York.

Ludwig, A. (2000) *Create an oasis with greywater*. 4th edn, Oasis Design, Santa Barbara, CA.

Lutzenhiser, L. (1990) Explaining consumption: the promises and limitations of energy and behaviour research. *Proceedings of the ACEEE 1990 Summer Study on Energy Efficiency in Buildings* **2**, p. 2.101.

Lynes, J.A. (1993) Analytical methods for daylighting design and performance prediction. *Proceedings of the CEC symposium 'Solar energy and buildings'*. Athens, 8–10 December 1993.

McConnell, J.V. (1986) *Understanding human behaviour*. 5th edn, Holt, Rinehart and Winston, New York.

McDowall, G.E. (1966) Report to the Honourable A.R. Fletcher, MLA Minister of Lands by the Inter-Departmental Committee on Leasing and Development of Queensland Islands, Queensland Government, Brisbane.

Macfarlane, W.V. (1959) *Thermal comfort zones*. Department of Physiology, University of Queensland, Brisbane.

McHarg, I.L. (1971) *Design with nature*. Doubleday, New York.

McHarg, I.L. (1971) *The environmental crisis Sydney*. Architecture in Australia (RAIA).

McIntyre, D.A. (1980) *Indoor climate*. Applied Science Publishers, London.

McMullan, R. (1992) *Environmental science in building*, 3rd edn. The Macmillan Press.

Macpherson, R.K. (1980) What makes people accept a thermal environment as comfortable?. In: Cowan, H.J. editor. *Solar energy applications in the design of buildings*. Applied Science Publishers, London.

Majoros, A. (1998) *Daylighting. PLEA Note* 4. Passive and Low Energy Architecture International, Brisbane.

Markus, T.A., and Morris, E.N. (1980) *Buildings, climate and energy*. Pitman, London.

Marland, B. (1994) The thermal performance of early Australian housing. *Proceedings of the 28th ANZAScA Conference.* Geelong, 26–28 September 1994, pp. 143–147.

Marsden, B.S. (ca.1973) Recent development on Queensland's resort islands. *The Australian Geographer.*

Marsh, A., and Carruthers, D. (1995) A selection of interactive design tools. *Proceedings of the 29th ANZAScA Conference.* Canberra, 11–13 July 1995, pp. 120–125.

Martin, H.A., and Peterson, J.A. (1978) Eustatic sea-level changes and environmental gradients. In: Pittock, A.B., Frakes, L.A., Jenssen, D., Peterson, J.A., and Zillman, J.W. editors., *Climatic change and variability: a southern perspective.* Cambridge University Press.

Mazria, E. (1979) *The passive solar energy book.* Emmaus, Rodale, Penn.

Mehta, H., Baez, A.L., and O'Loughlin, P. (eds.) (2002) *International ecolodge guidelines.* The International Eco-tourism Society, Burlington, VT.

Michelson, W. (1975) *Behavioral research methods in environmental design.* Dowden, Hutchinson & Ross, Stroudsburg, Penn.

Minnesota sustainable design guide (2000) University of Minnesota.

Moffar, A.S., and Schiler, M. (1981) *Landscape design that saves energy.* Morow, New York.

Mohajeri, R., and Fricke, F.R. (1995) An 'intelligent window' for minimising noise intrusion into building. *Proceedings of the 29th ANZAScA Conference.* Canberra, 11–13 July 1995, pp. 80–87.

Moore, J.E. (1967) *Design for good acoustics.* Architectural Press, London.

Morgan, C., and Stevenson, F. (2005) *Design for deconstruction.* Scottish Environment Protection Agency (SEDA).

National design handbook prototype on passive solar heating and natural cooling of buildings (1990) United Nations Centre for Human Settlements (Habitat), Nairobi.

National ecotourism strategy (1994) Australian Government Publishing Service, Canberra.

Nature and Ecotourism Accreditation Program, 2nd edn (2000) Brisbane: NEAP.

NEAP see Nature and Ecotourism Accreditation Program.

Nelson, P. (1994) Better guidance for better EIA. *Built Environment* **20**(4)(4): **280–293.**

Nicol, F. (1995) Climate and thermal comfort in India. In *Climatically responsive energy efficient architecture*, **1**, Center for Advanced Studies in Architecture, New Delhi, pp. 3.1–3.10.

Norton, J. (2000) *Sustainable architecture: a definition.* Habitat Debate viewed 23/3/2000 <www.unchs. org/unchs/english/hdv5n2/forum1.htm>.

Olgyay, V. (1963) (reprinted 1992) *Design with climate.* Van Nostrand Reinhold, New York.

Olgyay, V., and Olgyay, A. (1957) (reprinted 1976) *Solar control and shading devices.* Princeton University Press, Princeton, NJ.

Olweny, M.R.O. (1993) Thermal comfort studies in East Africa: Kampala, Uganda. *Proceedings of the 27th ANZAScA Conference.* Sydney, 12–14 November 1993, pp. 53–61.

Ortega, A., Rybczynski, W., Ayad, S., Ali, W., and Acheson, A. (1975) *The Ecol operation* 2nd rev. edn. Minimum Cost Housing Group, McGill University, Montreal.

Osland, G.E., and Mackoy, R. (2004) Ecolodge performance goals and evaluations. *Journal of Ecotourism* **3**(2)(2): **109–128.**

Owens, S.E., and Rickaby, P.A. (1992) Settlements and energy revisited. *Built Environment* **18**(4)(4): **247–252.**

Papanek, V. (1995) *The green imperative, ecology and ethics in design and architecture.* Thames and Hudson, London.

Passive solar design handbook (1980) US Department of Energy, Washington, DC.

Passive solar design – tropical & subtropical (1990) Cement and Concrete Association of Australia, North Sydney.

Paul Kernan Architect and Penner & Associates (2001) *Best practical guide: material choices for sustainable design.* Greater Vancouver Regional District viewed 30/5/2005 <gvrd.bc.ca/buildsmart>.

Pearce, D.G. (1987) *Tourism today: a geographical analysis.* Longman Scientific and Technical, Harlow.

Pearson, D. (1989) *The natural house book.* Angus & Robertson.

Pesaran, A.A. (1992) Impact of ambient pressure on performance of desiccant cooling systems. *Proceedings of the American Society of Mechanical Engineers conference 'Solar Engineering'* **1**, Hawaii, pp. 235–246.

Petherbridge, P. (1974) *Limiting the temperatures in naturally ventilated buildings in warm climates.* Building Research Establishment Current Paper 7/74 BRE Garston, Watford, UK.

Pilatowicz, G. (1995) *Eco-interiors: a guide to environmentally conscious interior design.* John Wiley & Sons, New York.

Phillips, R.O. (1951) *Sunshine and shade in Australia.* Commonwealth Experimental Building Station, Sydney.

Ponting, C. (1992) *A green history of the world.* Penguin Books, London.

Pressure, atmospheric/barometric, 71, 77
environmental, **4**, 22
vapour, **56**, 77, 78, 113
wind/air, 12, 70, 72, 73, **73**, 75, 107, 115
Preventative maintenance *see* maintenance
Privacy, acoustic, 50, 87, 88, 98, 111, 112, 115, **160**, 160, 163
visual, 50, 98, 115, 146, **148**, 163, 203, **205**
Psychological effects/impacts, 6, 50, 79, 80, 83, 87, 91, 92, 111
aspects/factors, 45, 53, 54, 57, 69, 83, 91, 92, 97, 99, 192
Psychometric chart, 55, **56**, 77
PV *see* photovoltaic panel(-s)

Quick thermal response, 69, 129, 169

R-value, 124
Radiant cooling *see* cooling, radiant
Radiation/ir-. solar, 12, 14, 16, 17, 50, 53, **56**, 58–60, **59**, **61**, 62–66, 74, 79–82, **84**, 101, 102, 102, 107, 109, 111, 114, 118, 122, 123, 160, 201 *see also* insolation
rainfall, 13–17, 13, 31, 101, 141 *see also* precipitation
Recycle(-ing), 8, 22, **23**, 31–37, **34**, 38, 39, 125, 145, 146, 149, 159, 160, 166, 178, 188, 195, 199, 200, 209, 211, 213, **213**, 214
Reduce(-ing, -tion), 5, 8, 17, 19, 22–27, **23**, 29, 31–34, **34**, 36–40, 43, 48, 55, 58, 59, 63, 65, 66, 68, 70, 71, 76, 79–82, 84, 88, 95, 101, 107, 109–111, 113, 114, **114**, 116, 118, **118**, 119, 122, 123, 126, 137, 139, 146, 149, 150, 155, 193, 195, 196, 200, 209, 213
Reflectance, 59, 122–124
Reflected light, 79, 81–83, 86, **86**, 118, 122
component (solar radiation), 58, **117**
Reflection (heat), 123
light, 79, 81, **84**, 86
sound, 88, 127
Reflective insulation, 63, 64, **114**, 122–123
Refrigerator(-tion), 12, 24, 28, 153, 185, 207
Regulations/regulatory measures, 43
Relative humidity (RH) *see* humidity, relative (RH)
Remote location, 7, 18, 23, 24, 28, 32, 55, 139
Renewable energy/energy sources, 5, 21, 23–25, 27–29, 36
materials, 125
Re-radiation, 122
Resistance, thermal (R), 82, 119, 121, 122, 124
Resistive insulation, 63, 122, 124
Response, behavioural, 5, 69

climatic/environmental, 5, 17, 18, 21, 22, 39, 95–99, 139
design, 9, 12, 15, 21, 22, 55, 57, 97, 99, 131, 133
physiological, 5, 54, 57, 76, 91, 97
psychological, 76, 87, 91
thermal, 66, 69, 109, 123
Return (investment), 145
Ridge/Venturi effect, 73, **74**, 114, **116**
vent(-s), **113**, 114, **116**
Risk(-s), 24, 25, 29, 40, 80, 133, 196
Roof angle/pitch/tilt, 31, 65, 73, **74**, 112, 156, 214
area, 59, 111, 114
cover/structure, 22, 38, 50, 62, 64, 75, 77, 85, 109, **113**, 114, **114**, 115, **115**, **117**, 120, 123, **123**, 124, 127, 141, 146, 147, **148**, **150**, 151, 155, 156, **167**, 169, **176**, 197
form(-s), **117**, 133, 137
monitor(-s) *see* monitor(-)/vent(-s), roof
orientation, 30
pond, 22, 64, 65, **65**
shading, 26, 58, 59, 102, 114
vent(-s) *see* monitor(-)/vent(-s), roof
Roof-integrated PV panel(-s), 26 *see also* photovoltaic(-s) (PV) panel(-s)
Roof, parasol *see* parasol/double-shell/umbrella roof
Room acoustics, 87–89, 133
unit/building volume, 57, 62, 67, 97, 114, 126, 129, **130**
Rubbish, 40, **177** *see also* waste
Rule(-s) of thumb, 79, **117**, 118, 127
Running costs *see* operational(-ing)/running costs

Saturation (humidity), 77
Screen(-s), acoustic, 88, 89 *see also* barrier(-s), acoustic/noise/sound
insect/fly- *see* fly-screen(-s)/insect screen(-s)
visual, 19, 81, 83 *see also* barrier(-s), visual
Sea (influence) *see* ocean/sea (influence)
Season(-al) change, 11, 15, 17, 27, 31, 47, 53, 55, 60, 68, 77, 78, 81, 95, 96, 111, 112, 114, 137, 141, 146, 197, 207, 213
Sensible heat, 60, 126, 151, **190**
Septic tank/system(-s), 31, 32, 166, 178, 185, 195, 209
Service(-s), building, 15, 21, 23–25, 30, **38**, 43, 45, 93, 101, 113
life, 37, 38
Sewage system, 31, 149, 160, 178, 188, 199
treatment, 31, 35, 159
Shade(-s)/sun-, window, 23, 57, 60, 82, 96, 111, **113**, **118**, 118, 123
Shading coefficient, 60
design, 57, 59, **84**, 96, **103**, 109, **113**, 116, **118**, 121, 129, 143, 151, 169, 178, 207

device(-s), 59, 60, 79, 81, 83, **83**, 84, 118, **118**
  with overhangs, **61**, **84**, **118**, 179
  with trees/vegetation, 60, **62**, 79, 81, **84**, 107, **117**, **118**, 147
  roof(-s) *see* roof shading
  site *see* site shading
  wall(-s) *see* wall shading
  window(-s)/opening(-s) *see* window shading
Shadow angle, horizontal/vertical, 60
Sink(-s) (heat), 17, 36, 57, 63, 64, **102**, 120, 122
Site analysis/considerations, 16, 133
  climate *see* microclimate
  conditions), 21, 23, 24, 32, 34, 40, 45, 60, 70, 72, 93, 101, 102
  design/plan(-ning), 24, 77, 88, 95, 97, 101, 102, 107, **147**, 154, **164**, **174**, 186, **194**, 196
  selection, 14, 58, 146, 153, 163, 176, 186, 196, 203, 211
  shading, 16, 60, **62**
Skytherm roof, 64
Slope(-s), 14, 17, 101
Sol-air temperature (SAT), 63
Solar architecture, 4
  cells *see* photovoltaic(-s) (PV) (panels)
  chimney *see* Chimney, solar
  control, 121
  energy, 26, 27, 58–60, 78, 145, 178
  (heat) gain(-s), 25, 58, 59, 63, 75, 81, 82, **85**, 114, 118, 122, 124, 129
  irradiation (insolation) *see* Radiation/ir-. solar
  water heater(-s), 29
  shade(-s) *see* Shade(-s)/sun-, window
Solid waste(-s), 33–35, 160, 166, 178, 188, 195, 199, 209, 214
Sound(-s), 29, 40, 47, 79, 87, 88, 89, **89**, 91, 95, 102, 116, 126, 127, 137, 138, 169, 210 *see also* noise
  barrier(-s) *see* barrier(-s), sound
  impact(-s)/effect(-s), 22, 88
  insulation, 88, **89**, 122, 127, **127**
  level(-s), 87, 88, 91, 97
  meter
  pollution, 26, 137, 210
  privacy *see* privacy, acoustic
  transmission, 88, **89**, 116, 127
  background *see* background noise/sound
Source(-s), heat/energy, 23, 24–28, **24**, **30**, 97, 147, 156, 166, 176, 178, 185, 187, **188**, 197, 213
  light, 79–82, 86, 91, 138
  sound, 87–89, 137, 138
  water, 31, 32, **32**, 99, 159
Space air conditioning *see* air-conditioning
Specific heat, 66, 101, 126
  volume, 55
spectrum (light), 79, 82

(sound), 29, 87
Specular reflection, 79, 81, 123
Speed, air/wind *see* velocity/speed, wind/air flow
Stack effect, 68, 70, 72, **72**, 74, 75, 112, 187, **190**
Stand-alone system(-s) (power), 24
Standard effective temperature (SET), 77
Statistical data/statistics, 15, 54
Steady-state (heat flow), 66
Steam (energy source), 26
Storage capacity (energy), 26, 126
Storm water, 31, 33
Stress, heat/thermal, 1, 15, 16, 53, 55–57, 69, 71, 77, 78, 91
Structure, heavy-weight *see* heavy(-weight) construction/materials
  light-weight *see* light(-weight) construction/ materials
Sun path, 60
Sunlight, 26, 79–84, 86, 91, 99, 123, 137 *see also* daylight
Sunshade(-s) *see* Shade(-s)/sun-, window
Supply, air *see* air provision/supply
  fuel, 26, 27, 139
  energy/power, 21, 23, 25, 27–29, 185, 187, 193
  water *see* water supply
Surface (material characteristics), 36, 58–60, 62, 63, 64, 66, 76, 79, 80, 83, 84, **84**, 86, 87, **89**, 91, 102, 104, 114, 115, **118**, 122, 123, 127
  colour *see* colour (material characteristics)
  conductance/resistance (heat flow), 63, **71**, 124
  temperature, 63, **66**, **67**, 69, **102**, **117**, 122, **123**, 123
Sustainability, **30**, 98, 145, 146, 193
Sustainable architecture/building(-s)/design, 3–6, 21, 38, 44, 145
  development, 40, 43
  resource(-s), 27, 31, 32, 36, 44
  tourism, 7–8, 43
Swing, diurnal (temperature) *see* diurnal swing/ range (temperature)

Temperature, 1, 11, 12, 14–17, 26–28, 45, 47–50, 53–59, **56**, **58**, 62–70, **66**, **67**, **68**, **70**, 72, 76–78, 86, 91, 92, 95, 99, 101, 102, **102**, 107, 109, **114**, 114, 115, 117, **117**, 120–124, **123**, 126, 129– 131, **131**, 141–143, 150, 151, 160, 166, **169**, 169, 178, 187, 188, 192, 200
  air, 11, 12, 47, 49, 55, 56, **56**, 63, 65, 68–70, **70**, 72, 77, 78, 91, 101, **102**, 122, 141, 142
  average, 13, **13**, 16, 55, 66, **67**, 68, 77, 78, 126, 131, 142, 143
  constant, 1, 27
  difference, 63, 64, 72, 109, 123, 124

Temperature (cont.)
  dry bulb *see* dry bulb temperature (DBT)
  gradient, 68, 74, 113
  ground/under-ground, 67, **67**, 77, 126
  indoor/internal, 48, 54, 66, **66**, 68, 69, 109, 114,
    117, 141, 143, 160, 166, 178, 192, 200, 210, 214
  maximum, 13, **13**, 16, 56–58, 65, 66, 142
  mean, 11–13, 15, 16, 54–57, 67 *see also* mean
    radiant temperature (MRT)
  minimum, 13, **13**, 16, 55, 68, 101, 141–143
  monthly, 16, 54, 55
  outdoor/external, 55, 59, 68, 109, 129, 131, 141,
    150, 160, 166, 178, 188, 200, 209, 214
  Sol-air *see* Sol-air temperature (SAT)
  stratification, vertical, 75
  swing/range, diurnal *see* diurnal (temperature)
    swing/range
  (psychological effect of sound) *see* psychological
    effects/impacts
Thermal balance, 48, 54, 57
  capacity, 66, 68, 126
  comfort, 43, 47–49, 53–55, **70**, 71, 76–79, 91, 92,
    126
  conditions, 16, 112, 131, 141, 156
  control, 111
  environment, 45, 48, 49, 53, 55, **58**, 88, 91, 118,
    133, **150**, **156**, **196**
  geothermal energy, 27
  mass, 66, 68, 109, 121, 122, 126, 179, 187, **197**, 200
  neutrality, 54, 55, 131, 143
  performance *see* performance, thermal
  system, 69
Thermoregulation, 49, 91
Tidal energy, 27
Tilt angle, 58, 60, 107
Timber (building material), 34, 35, 38, 39, 59, 69,
    71, 76, 83, 84, 124, 146, 154, 155, 163, **165**,
    176, 197, 203, 213
Time (period), 1, 12, 13, 15, 26, 28, 36–38, 47, 48,
    50, 57, 58, 63, **66**, **67**, **68**, 75, 76, 78, 80, 81, 83,
    86, 92, 95, 96, 98, 99, 109, 114, 125, 129–131,
    130, 137, 139, 141, 144, 149, 161, **186**, 215
    see also daytime; night-time
  lag, 63, 66, **66**, **67**, 68, 109, 151, 169, 178
Topography, 14–16, 45, 60, 97, 99, 101, 103, 141
Topsoil, 34
Town (water) mains, 159, 166, 178
Traffic, 15, 20, 154
Transmission (electricity), 25, 29
  heat, 66, 117, 123, 124
  light *see* light transmission
  loss, sound (STL), 116
  sound *see* sound transmission
Transmittance *see* U-value

Transmitted radiation, 58
Transparent/-cy, 59, **61**, 64, 82, 122
Trees, 34, 35, 153, 154, 176, 186, 195, 196, 211, 215
    see also biodiversity; 'green corridors'; plants;
    vegetation
  (airflows), 74, 102, **104**, 107, 114 *see also* plants;
    vegetation
  (shade), 50, 59, 101, 102, 104, 107, 114, 118, 214
    see also plants; vegetation
Trombe (Trombe-Michel) wall, 75, **75**
Tube(-s), underground *see* pipe(-s)/tube(-s),
    underground
Turbine(-s), 26–29, 86, 137, 185, 187, **187**, 197

U-value, 124
Ultra-sound, 26, 29
Underground tubes/pipes *see* pipe(-s)/tube(-s),
    underground

Vapour pressure, **56**, 77, 78, 113
Vegetation, 14, 15, 41, 98, 99, 101, 161, 176 *see also*
    biodiversity; 'green corridors'; plants, trees
  conservation, 19, 34, 40, 137, 196 *see also* biodi-
    versity; 'green corridors'; plants; trees
  dam(-s), **105** *see also* wind wing wall(-s)
  (influence/impacts), 12, 15, 17, 19, 58, 73, 76,
    86–88, 96, 102, 105, 107, 108, 119, 138, 151,
    160, 203 *see also* biodiversity; 'green corridors';
    plants; trees
  (shading), 19, 58, 60, **62**, 79, 81, **85**, 101, 103,
    117, 147 *see also* plants; trees
Velocity/speed, wind/air flow, 14–16, 26, 47, 53, **56**,
    70–74, **70**, **71**, **72**, **74**, 76, 101–103, **103**, **104**,
    120, 123
Ventilation, 21, 24, 55, 57, 59, 66, **68**, 69, 72, **72**,
    76, **76**, 83, 88, 93, 95, 102, 103, 109, 115,
    117, 118, 126, 151, 160, 161, **168**, 169, 178,
    195, 214
  cross-, 63, 68, 69, 72, **72**, **73**, 87, 103, **103**, 111,
    112, 129, 133, 139, 143, 179, 187, 189
  pressure-driven, 73, **73**, **103**, 114, **116**, **190**
Vent(-s), roof *see* monitor(-)/vent(-s), roof
Visual environment, 22, 79, 80, 86, 149
  impact(-s), 22, 23, 25, 26, 79
  pollution, 29
  screen(-s) *see* screen(-s), visual
Volume, room *see* room/unit/building volume

Wall (acoustic barrier) *see* barrier(-s), acoustic/noise/
    sound
  shading, 56, 58, 59, **60**, **61**, **84**, 115, **117**, **118**, 156

Warm-humid climate(-s), 11 *see also* hot-humid climate(-s)

Waste, 3, 9, 21–23, **23**, 25, 29, 31–36, 34, 38, 39, 43, 137, 143, 146, 149, 150, 159, 160, 166, 178, 185, 188, 193, 195, 199, 200, 209, 213, 214 *see also* rubbish

Wastewater, 22, 31–33, 32, 36, 149 *see also* liquid waste

Water conservation, 22, 31, 32, 36, 146, 149, 213
  consumption, 31, 32, 159, 178, 188, 195, 199
  (energy source), 25, 27, 28, 30, 147
  heating, 21, 24, 25, 28, 29, 33, 156, **157**, 197, **198** *see also* solar water heater(-ing)
  potable, 21, 32, 195
  supply, 21, 23, 27, 31, 32, 185, 186
  treatment, 31 *see also* leach field

Wavelength (solar radiation), 64, 80, 122
  (sound), 87

Weather, 15, 56, 71, 77, 81, 97, 99, 101, 139, 143, 144, 192, 210, 214
  conditions, 25, 99, **197**
  data *see* climate/climatic/meteorological data
  station *see* meteorological station(-s)

Wet bulb temperature (WBT), 12, 55, **56**, 65, 66, 77

'White' noise *see* background/masking noise/sound

Wind (energy source), 21, 24–26, 28–30, **30**, 147, 185, 187, **187**, 193, 197
  direction, 16, 73, 102, 103, **103**
  turbines, 29, 86, **185**, 187, **187**, 197
  velocity/speed gradient, 74, **74** *see also* velocity/ speed, wind/air flow
  wing wall(-s), 60, **107** *see also* vegetation dam(-s)

Window(-s), 5, 23, 47, 59, 60, 76, 80–82, 88, 96, 111, 112, 117, 118, 119, 122, 123, 133, 138, 141, 147, **150**, 153, 179, 187 *see also* fenestration; opening(-s)
  shading, 59, 118, **118**

Wood (energy source), 23

Zenith (solar), 11, 58, 101

Zone/-ing (building), 72, 88, 118
  coastal, 14–17, **18**, 101
  comfort, 55, **56**, 78, 109
  (region/area), 1, 11, **14**, 15–17, 19, 50, 53–55, 96, 98, 99, 101, 109
  (site), 29, 39, 68, 72, 88, 107, 154